THE *Yachting* BOOK OF CELESTIAL NAVIGATION

ALSO BY STAFFORD CAMPBELL

THE *YACHTING* BOOK OF COASTWISE NAVIGATION

THE *Yachting* BOOK OF CELESTIAL NAVIGATION

Stafford Campbell

DODD, MEAD & COMPANY New York

Published by Dodd, Mead & Company, Inc.
79 Madison Avenue, New York, N.Y. 10016
Distributed in Canada by
McClelland and Stewart Limited, Toronto
Manufactured in the United States of America
Designed by Stanley S. Drate/Folio Graphics Co., Inc.
First Edition

Library of Congress Cataloging in Publication Data

Campbell, Stafford.
The yachting book of celestial navigation.

Includes index.
1. Nautical astronomy. 2. Navigation. 3. Yachts and
yachting. I. Title.
VK555.C23 1984 623.89 84-6079
ISBN 0-396-08388-9 (pbk.)

Contents

Abbreviations Commonly Used in Celestial Navigation

a	Altitude difference, or intercept
***a*λ**	Assumed longitude
***a*L**	Assumed latitude
A	Away
AP	Assumed position
corr	Correction to a tabulated value
d	Declination hourly change, or tabular altitude differential
D	Dip; correction for observer's height of eye
Dec (dec)	Declination of a celestial body
DR	Dead reckoning (position)
GHA (gha)	Greenwich hour angle
GMT	Greenwich mean time
GP	Geographical position (of a celestial body on earth)
ha (App. Alt.)	Apparent altitude
hs	Sextant altitude
Hc	Computed altitude
Ho	Observed altitude
H.P.	Horizontal parallax
IC	Index correction

incr	Incremental value
L	Lower limb
LAN	Local apparent noon
LHA	Local hour angle
Mer Pass	Meridian passage (time of)
R	Refraction corrections
SHA	Sidereal hour angle
T	Toward
Tab	Tabular value
U	Upper limb
UTC	Coordinated universal time
v	Small, variable corrections
W	Watch time
z	Zenith distance
Z	Uncorrected azimuth angle
ZD	Zone description
Zn	True azimuth
♈	First point of Aries (Vernal Equinox)
°	Degrees
′	Minutes (of arc)

Introduction

"What can be more difficult than to guide a ship when only water and heaven may be seen?" So said the distinguished Spanish geographer, Martín Cortés, in the introduction to his celebrated navigational work in 1551. But times have changed; we live in the late twentieth century, and with the technical developments that have taken place since Cortés's day, celestial navigation has now become as easy as piloting. Finding one's way on the open sea by means of the heavenly array is, in fact, a logical extension of the technique of coastwise piloting, the most notable difference being that celestial bodies are constantly in motion relative to the observer, while charted, terrestrial objects remain stationary.

Why should one learn celestial navigation in these modern times? Aren't we living in the electronic age, where position finding is supposed to be a mere matter of pushing buttons? It is true that, within their limits, some of the marvelous new devices, such as radio direction-finders, or Loran, or satellite navigators, may be as useful offshore as they are in coastal waters, but it is equally true that, like any electronic device, they can never be entirely immune to failure, particularly in the environment of a yacht at sea. Celestial navigation, being self-contained and dependent only on the navigator, therefore remains as the ultimate backup—the one method that will bring you home when all else fails. At the same time, there is an extraordinary personal satisfaction in knowing that you can pinpoint your position at sea, using similar tools and sighting the same sun, moon, and stars as did the great navigators of history. For many of us, that satisfaction is reason enough to rely on celestial as our primary means of offshore navigation.

This book starts with the assumption that you are already familiar with the fundamentals of piloting. Should you feel out-of-practice, I can recommend our companion volume, *The Yachting Book of Coastwise Navigation,* as a refresher. In addition to the charts, protractor, and dividers you have used in piloting, there are only a few more tools needed for celestial navigation: a sextant for making the observation; a watch for timing it; and an almanac and sight reduction table for converting the sight into a line of position.

The system taught here (based upon the *Nautical Almanac* and DMA Pub. No. 249) is the fastest and easiest tabular system that is available today. Its accuracy is entirely compatible with that of observations made from a yacht, and the speed of solution, in the hands of a capable navigator, is comparable to that of a manual calculator. The most sophisticated calculators—those programmed specifically to solve celestial problems—may be still faster, and for those interested, we will explore their use as a substitute for the tables, in Chapter 12. Always remember, however, that calculators possess the same frailties as other delicate electronic instruments, and every prudent navigator should acquire a thorough understanding of the tabular method as a precautionary measure in case of equipment failure.

There are two basic approaches to learning celestial navigation. Traditionally, the theory of celestial mechanics was mastered first, and only then did the practical experience begin. The opposite approach, and the one I prefer, is to start with practical exposure—picking up the sextant and making an actual observation—and then, after having learned the technique, you can review the underlying theory if you're interested. I subscribe to the principle that one doesn't have to understand the theory of the internal-combustion engine to be able to drive an automobile; that practical experience is much more important. Accordingly, I have devoted Chapters 1–6 to the practice of taking and solving a sun sight—just as you would do it aboard a yacht—and that process is extended in Chapters 7, 8, and 9 to include the moon, the planets, and the stars. Chapter 11 contains an explanation of the fundamentals of celestial theory, but if you feel you want still more background, the classic texts, "Bowditch" *(American Practical Navigator)*, and "Dutton" *(Dutton's Navigation & Piloting)* are ideal for reference.

In piloting, besides plotting courses and keeping track of the dead reckoning position, you learned how to take bearings on fixed objects, such as lighthouses or prominent landmarks, and how to plot those bearings as lines of position on your chart. You will also recall that the intersection of two or more of the position lines produced a fix, independent of any previous position. A bearing obtained by a radio direction-finder, radar, or by other electronic means produces a similar line of position, one that can be used in exactly the same manner as, and in conjunction with, lines obtained visually. The position line doesn't even have to be a straight line. A distance-off measurement, for example, produces a curve—part of the circumference of the circle whose radius is the distance off—and a Loran line has a characteristic hyperbolic shape.

The key concept is that of the *line of position,* which Bowditch defines as "a line on some point of which a vessel may be presumed to be located as a result of observation or measurement." You are well on your way to taking the mystery out of celestial navigation when you realize that the result of a celestial observation is simply another line of position, and that the lines obtained by this method are no different than any other position lines, and can be used in all the same ways.

Leaving the theory until later, let's review the six easy steps that are involved, from the time you select the celestial body to "shoot," to the plotting of the resulting line of position on your chart.

- Making the sextant observation
- Taking the time of the sight
- Extracting data from the almanac
- Calculating the computed altitude
- Determining intercept and azimuth
- Plotting the line of position

In celestial navigation, as in any specialized human activity, practitioners have built up a vocabulary over the years, which is often unintelligible to a layman. But don't despair; I'll give you a working definition of the commonly used terms as we go along, and, for ready reference, there is a glossary at the back of the book. The preface contains a list of abbreviations that are used for the principal terms. All of this nomenclature will become clearer when you see the practical purpose it serves, so, take your sextant in your right hand, and your watch in your left, and let's get started.

THE Yachting BOOK OF CELESTIAL NAVIGATION

1 The Sextant Observation: The Sun

The sextant observation is the one part of the celestial process in which the navigator's personal skill plays an essential role in its success, and this is especially true when the sight is made from the bouncing deck of a small boat. It has been said that the rest of the procedure has been reduced to "telephone-book arithmetic," which I can leave to you to judge, but becoming proficient in using a sextant is a question of practice—a true case of learning by doing.

A great deal has been written about the subtleties of selecting a sextant, but I have been able to achieve acceptable results with a plastic, lifeboat sextant, as well as with a brass instrument made in the mid-1800s for the clipper-ship trade. I have navigated halfway around the world with a Navy Mark 2 from World War II, and have sailed the other half with a modern C. Plath that is one of the finest available. My conclusion is that you can get a sound grounding in the fundamentals with almost any workable instrument, and your final selection can wait until you have accumulated enough practice to be able to make a personal judgment.

All modern marine sextants are similar in concept, based on the double-reflecting-mirror precept first suggested by Sir Isaac Newton in 1700. The principal parts are illustrated in Figure 1–1.

The purpose of the sextant is to make precise measurements of the altitude (the angular distance above the horizon) of a celestial body. The actual measuring is done by sighting the horizon through the clear portion of the horizon mirror, and then, by adjusting the sextant's movable index arm, the reflected image of the observed body is brought into coincidence with the horizon line. The altitude is read in whole degrees on the scale of the main

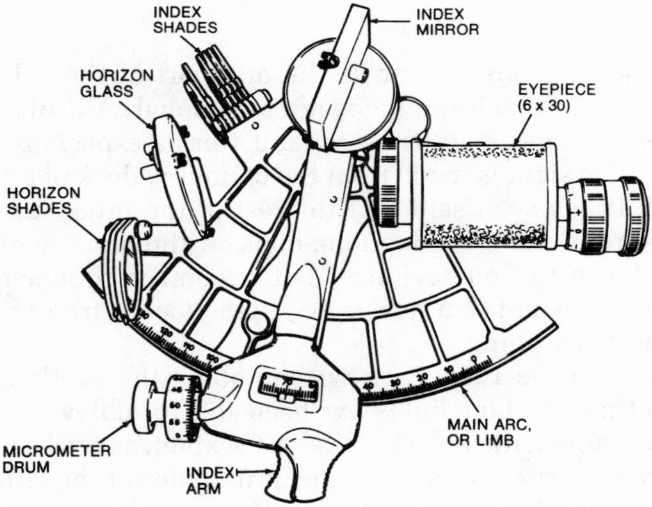

Figure 1–1. **The Principal Parts of a Modern Marine Sextant**

arc, or limb, and in fractional parts by means of the auxiliary scale—on the model illustrated, on the micrometer drum.

Sextants come with two varieties of horizon glasses: the conventional, half-silvered kind, in which the horizon is viewed through the clear half, and the body's reflected image in the mirrored half; and the new "whole-horizon" glass, in which the entire surface is both transparent and reflective, like a one-way mirror. Modern sextants are equipped with two sets of shades. The index shades are essential in an observation of the sun, because the intensity of the reflected image can cause injury to the unprotected eye. The horizon shades are designed to reduce the glare if the horizon appears to be too bright, thereby aiding the task of taking precise measurements. Whatever model you choose, remember that your sextant is a precision optical instrument, and proper care is a key to its performance. The two main enemies of a sextant aboard a yacht are the damp, salt-laden atmosphere, and exposure to physical shock. While the risk of damage can never be eliminated entirely, it can be substantially reduced by keeping the instrument protected from salt spray, to the extent possible, and by always returning it to its case, and stowing the case securely between sights. I suggest to beginners that they treat their sextants like fine china; then they will be ready to perform properly when needed.

Let's start first with a simple sun sight, probably the sight you will take more often than all others combined. This is not to discourage you in any way from trying the other celestial bodies—in fact, your technique will profit by it—but I recommend starting with the sun and learning it well, since it will be your constant companion. Let's assume we are off the New England coast on a fine, clear summer day, say, June 8, 1984, and you have come on deck just before noon to take your first sight. Holding the sextant in your right hand, swing down the darkest of the index shades, and, looking through the eyepiece, sight the horizon through the horizon glass. Then, moving the index arm with your left hand, bring the reflected image of the sun in the mirrored portion of the horizon glass down to the horizon line at which you have been aiming. Shifting your left hand to the micrometer drum, or to other means of fine adjustment, bring the sun's bottom edge—its "lower limb"—into exact coincidence with the visible horizon.

You will find that it takes less time to do it than to tell about it, but an experienced navigator will take a second or two more to rotate the sextant about the line of sight to the horizon, simply to make sure that the reflected image is at the very lowest part of its apparent arc, and that the sextant is being held absolutely vertically. Figure 1–2 illustrates the technique, known as rocking the sextant. This is how the sun's image would appear in a circular horizon glass as the sextant is being rocked. The instrument will be exactly vertical at the lowest part of the arc described, and that is the point where the altitude measurement should be made. Some sextants are equipped with a prism device attached to the horizon glass, giving the observer an indication if the instrument is not being held correctly, but however you check it, the altitude will be incorrectly high if the sight is not taken in a true vertical plane.

Traditionally, sextant altitudes are expressed in degrees (°), minutes (′), and tenths of minutes. The angular measurement from the horizon to your zenith, directly overhead, is 90°00′. There are 60 minutes of arc in each whole degree, and 60 seconds in each minute, although tenths of minutes are more commonly used in celestial navigation. You shouldn't have any difficulty reading your sextant, but to avoid careless errors, it's always a good idea to read the whole degrees first from the main

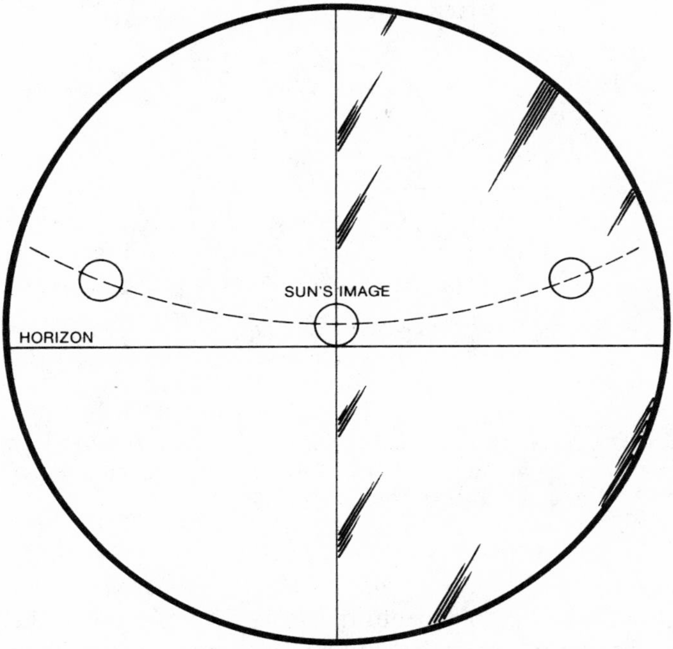

Figure 1–2. **Rocking the Sextant. The sun's image appears to describe an arc in the horizon glass when the sextant is rotated about the line of sight to the horizon. The correct altitude is measured at the lowest point of the arc.**

arc, and then the minutes and any fractions from the micrometer drum or vernier. The sextant illustrated in Figure 1–3, set for the hypothetical sun sight you have just taken, reads 69° on the main arc, 48′ on the micrometer drum, and 0.5′ on its vernier. The sextant altitude is, therefore, 69°48.5′, or, as it is abbreviated by navigators, 69–48.5.

Having determined the sextant altitude (hs), it must be corrected for such things as errors that might be

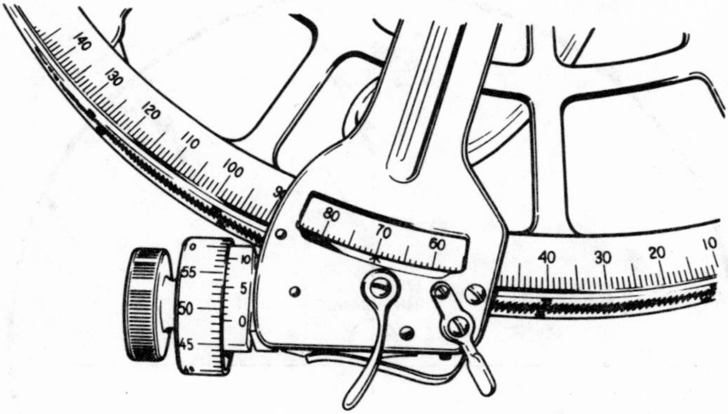

Figure 1-3. **Reading the Sextant. Whole degrees are read from the main arc, or limb; minutes and tenths from the micrometer drum or vernier. The reading illustrated is 69°48.5′.**

inherent in the instrument, the difference between the line of sight to your visible horizon and the true horizontal, and for the bending of light rays as they travel through the earth's atmosphere; small corrections, to be sure, but important for accuracy in your sight calculations. The first correction, called the index correction (IC), is necessary because even the finest sextant cannot be expected to stay in perfect adjustment. IC is determined before or after taking a sight by setting the index arm at zero degrees and aiming the sextant at the horizon. The horizon line may appear to be slightly offset between the clear and the reflecting portions of the horizon glass. Using the fine adjustment, the horizon line is brought back into coincidence, and the sextant read. The correction needed to bring that reading back to zero is the index correction. It is good practice to check the IC each time a sextant is used, but one check will suffice for a simultaneous series of sights. In our exercise, let's say that you checked your sextant just before shooting the sun, and found that when the horizon line was exactly straight the instrument read 2.4′, not zero. Then, IC is *minus* 2.4′, the amount necessary to bring the reading back to zero.

The second correction is for dip (D). This is to compensate for the slight difference in the angle between the true horizontal and the line of sight to the horizon as you view it from your elevated position on deck. The effect of dip is to cause the measured altitude to be too high, so that the correction, based on the observer's height of eye above the surface, is always negative. The value of the D-correction is taken from the DIP column in the almanac's altitude correction tables, an example of which is shown in Figure 1–4.

The altitude tables are of a type called critical tables; that is, a table in which a single value is tabulated for all readings between limiting entry values. Referring to the excerpt from the dip table in Figure 1–5, for your height of eye at the time of your sun sight, which, let's assume, was 9 feet, the D-correction would be –2.9′, the correction for all heights of eye between 8.6 and 9.2 feet.

Taking the net total of the IC and D-corrections, and applying that to the sextant altitude, you arrive at an intermediate value called apparent altitude (ha). This value is then used to find the third and final altitude correction, the refraction, or R-correction. In our example, the IC of –2.4′, and the D-correction of –2.9′ total –5.3′ which, when applied to the hs of 69°48.5′, produces an ha of 69°43.2′.

To determine the final altitude correction, enter the SUN column of the almanac tables, a portion of which is shown in Figure 1–6. Strictly speaking, the almanac designers have lumped several corrections together, all of which depend on the apparent altitude, so, for convenience, we can deal with them all as a single correction.

ALTITUDE CORRECTION TABLES 10°-90°—SUN, STARS, PLANETS

SUN

OCT.—MAR. App. Alt.	Lower Limb	Upper Limb	APR.—SEPT. App. Alt.	Lower Limb	Upper Limb
9 34	10·8	21·5	9 39	10·6	21·2
9 45	10·9	21·4	9 51	10·7	21·1
9 56	11·0	21·3	10 03	10·8	21·0
10 08	11·1	21·2	10 15	10·9	20·9
10 21	11·2	21·1	10 27	11·0	20·8
10 34	11·3	21·0	10 40	11·1	20·7
10 47	11·4	20·9	10 54	11·2	20·6
11 01	11·5	20·8	11 08	11·3	20·5
11 15	11·6	20·7	11 23	11·4	20·4
11 30	11·7	20·6	11 38	11·5	20·3
11 46	11·8	20·5	11 54	11·6	20·2
12 02	11·9	20·4	12 10	11·7	20·1
12 19	12·0	20·3	12 28	11·8	20·0
12 37	12·1	20·2	12 46	11·9	19·9
12 55	12·2	20·1	13 05	12·0	19·8
13 14	12·3	20·0	13 24	12·1	19·7
13 35	12·4	19·9	13 45	12·2	19·6
13 56	12·5	19·8	14 07	12·3	19·5
14 18	12·6	19·7	14 30	12·4	19·4
14 42	12·7	19·6	14 54	12·5	19·3
15 06	12·8	19·5	15 19	12·6	19·2
15 32	12·9	19·4	15 46	12·7	19·1
15 59	13·0	19·3	16 14	12·8	19·0
16 28	13·1	19·2	16 44	12·9	18·9
16 59	13·2	19·1	17 15	13·0	18·8
17 32	13·3	19·0	17 48	13·1	18·7
18 06	13·4	18·9	18 24	13·2	18·6
18 42	13·5	18·8	19 01	13·3	18·5
19 21	13·6	18·7	19 42	13·4	18·4
20 03	13·7	18·6	20 25	13·5	18·3
20 48	13·8	18·5	21 11	13·6	18·2
21 35	13·9	18·4	22 00	13·7	18·1
22 26	14·0	18·3	22 54	13·8	18·0
23 22	14·1	18·2	23 51	13·9	17·9
24 21	14·2	18·1	24 53	14·0	17·8
25 26	14·3	18·0	26 00	14·1	17·7
26 36	14·4	17·9	27 13	14·2	17·6
27 52	14·5	17·8	28 33	14·3	17·5
29 15	14·6	17·7	30 00	14·4	17·4
30 46	14·7	17·6	31 35	14·5	17·3
32 26	14·8	17·5	33 20	14·6	17·2
34 17	14·9	17·4	35 17	14·7	17·1
36 20	15·0	17·3	37 26	14·8	17·0
38 36	15·1	17·2	39 50	14·9	16·9
41 08	15·2	17·1	42 31	15·0	16·8
43 59	15·3	17·0	45 31	15·1	16·7
47 10	15·4	16·9	48 55	15·2	16·6
50 46	15·5	16·8	52 44	15·3	16·5
54 49	15·6	16·7	57 02	15·4	16·4
59 23	15·7	16·6	61 51	15·5	16·3
64 30	15·8	16·5	67 17	15·6	16·2
70 12	15·9	16·4	73 16	15·7	16·1
76 26	16·0	16·3	79 43	15·8	16·0
83 05	16·1	16·2	86 32	15·9	15·9
90 00			90 00		

STARS AND PLANETS

App. Alt.	Corrn
9 56	5·3
10 08	5·2
10 20	5·1
10 33	5·0
10 46	4·9
11 00	4·8
11 14	4·7
11 29	4·6
11 45	4·5
12 01	4·4
12 18	4·3
12 35	4·2
12 54	4·1
13 13	4·0
13 33	3·9
13 54	3·8
14 16	3·7
14 40	3·6
15 04	3·5
15 30	3·4
15 57	3·3
16 26	3·2
16 56	3·1
17 28	3·0
18 02	2·9
18 38	2·8
19 17	2·7
19 58	2·6
20 42	2·5
21 28	2·4
22 19	2·3
23 13	2·2
24 11	2·1
25 14	2·0
26 22	1·9
27 36	1·8
28 56	1·7
30 24	1·6
32 00	1·5
33 45	1·4
35 40	1·3
37 48	1·2
40 08	1·1
42 44	1·0
45 36	0·9
48 47	0·8
52 18	0·7
56 11	0·6
60 28	0·5
65 08	0·4
70 11	0·3
75 34	0·2
81 13	0·1
87 03	0·0
90 00	

App. Alt.	Additional Corrn
1984	
VENUS	
Jan. 1-Dec. 12	
0	
	+ 0·1
60	
Dec. 13-Dec. 31	
0	
	+ 0·2
41	
	+ 0·1
76	
MARS	
Jan. 1-Mar. 4	
0	
	+ 0·1
60	
Mar. 5-Apr. 24	
0	
	+ 0·2
41	
	+ 0·1
76	
Apr. 25-June 15	
0	
	+ 0·3
34	
	+ 0·2
60	
	+ 0·1
80	
June 16-Aug. 27	
0	
	+ 0·2
41	
	+ 0·1
76	
Aug. 28-Dec. 31	
0	
	+ 0·1
60	

DIP

Ht. of Eye (m)	Corrn	Ht. of Eye (ft.)
2·4		8·0
	2·8	
2·6		8·6
	2·9	
2·8		9·2
	3·0	
3·0		9·8
	3·1	
3·2		10·5
	3·2	
3·4		11·2
	3·3	
3·6		11·9
	3·4	
3·8		12·6
	3·5	
4·0		13·3
	3·6	
4·3		14·1
	3·7	
4·5		14·9
	3·8	
4·7		15·7
	3·9	
5·0		16·5
	4·0	
5·2		17·4
	4·1	
5·5		18·3
	4·2	
5·8		19·1
	4·3	
6·1		20·1
	4·4	
6·3		21·0
	4·5	
6·6		22·0
	4·6	
6·9		22·9
	4·7	
7·2		23·9
	4·8	
7·5		24·9
	4·9	
7·9		26·0
	5·0	
8·2		27·1
	5·1	
8·5		28·1
	5·2	
8·8		29·2
	5·3	
9·2		30·4
	5·4	
9·5		31·5
	5·5	
9·9		32·7
	5·6	
10·3		33·9
	5·7	
10·6		35·1
	5·8	
11·0		36·3
	5·9	
11·4		37·6
	6·0	
11·8		38·9
	6·1	
12·2		40·1
	6·2	
12·6		41·5
	6·3	
13·0		42·8
	6·4	
13·4		44·2
	6·5	
13·8		45·5
	6·6	
14·2		46·9
	6·7	
14·7		48·4
	6·8	
15·1		49·8
	6·9	
15·5		51·3
	7·0	
16·0		52·8
	7·1	
16·5		54·3
	7·2	
16·9		55·8
	7·3	
17·4		57·4
	7·4	
17·9		58·9
	7·5	
18·4		60·5
	7·6	
18·8		62·1
	7·7	
19·3		63·8
	7·8	
19·8		65·4
	7·9	
20·4		67·1
	8·0	
20·9		68·8
	8·1	
21·4		70·5

Ht. of Eye	Corrn
m	
1·0	1·8
1·5	2·2
2·0	2·5
2·5	2·8
3·0	3·0
See table	
m	
20	7·9
22	8·3
24	8·6
26	9·0
28	9·3
30	9·6
32	10·0
34	10·3
36	10·6
38	10·8
40	11·1
42	11·4
44	11·7
46	11·9
48	12·2
ft.	
2	1·4
4	1·9
6	2·4
8	2·7
10	3·1
See table ←	
ft.	
70	8·1
75	8·4
80	8·7
85	8·9
90	9·2
95	9·5
100	9·7
105	9·9
110	10·2
115	10·4
120	10·6
125	10·8
130	11·1
135	11·3
140	11·5
145	11·7
150	11·9
155	12·1

Note: App. Alt. = Apparent altitude = Sextant altitude corrected for index error and dip.

Figure 1–4.* Example of Altitude Correction Tables from the *Nautical Almanac

DIP

Ht. of Eye	Corrn	Ht. of Eye
m		ft.
2·4		8·0
	2·8	
2·6		8·6
	2·9	
2·8		9·2
	3·0	
3·0		9·8
	3·1	
3·2		10·5
	3·2	
3·4		11·2
	3·3	
3·6		11·9
	3·4	
3·8		12·6
	3·5	
4·0		13·3
	3·6	
4·3		14·1
	3·7	
4·5		14·9
	3·8	
4·7		15·7
	3·9	

Ht. of Eye	Corr
m	
1·0	1·8
1·5	2·2
2·0	2·5
2·5	2·8
3·0	3·0
See table	
m	
20	7·9
22	8·3
24	8·6
26	9·0

Figure 1–5. **Excerpt from the DIP table showing the D-correction of – 2.9′ for a height of eye of 9 feet**

Having shot the sun in June, enter the APR.-SEPT. column under "Lower Limb," and with the ha of 69°43.2′, find the R-correction of +15.6′ between the appropriate critical values. Notice that we were careful to use the lower-limb values; had we brought the upper limb (the top of the sun's disc) to the horizon, the correction would have been –16.2′ for the same apparent altitude—a substantial difference if one is in error. Adding the +15.6′-correction to our apparent altitude, we have determined the "observed altitude" (Ho)—in our case, 69°58.8′—which we will set aside while we proceed with the next three steps.

Every navigator worth his salt keeps a workbook, and one handy way to do this is with standardized forms which provide headings for prompting, and boxes for recording figures as they are obtained, thus providing

ALTITUDE CORRECTION TABLES 10°-90°

OCT.—MAR.	SUN		APR.—SEPT.		
App. Alt.	Lower Limb	Upper Limb	App. Alt.	Lower Limb	Upper Limb
9 34			9 39		
	+10·8	−21·5		+10·6	−21·2
9 45			9 51		
	+10·9	−21·4		+10·7	−21·1
9 56			10 03		
	+11·0	−21·3		+10·8	−21·0
10 08			10 15		
	+11·1	−21·2		+10·9	−20·9
10 21			10 27		
	+11·2	−21·1		+11·0	−20·8
10 34			10 40		
	+11·3	−21·0		+11·1	−20·7
10 47			10 54		
	+11·4	−20·9		+11·2	−20·6
11 01			11 08		
	+11·5	−20·8		+11·3	−20·5
11 15			11 23		
	+11·6	−20·7		+11·4	−20·4
11 30			11 38		
	+11·7	−20·6		+11·5	−20·3
11 46			11 54		
	+11·8	−20·5		+11·6	−20·2
43 59			45 31		
	+15·3	−17·0		+15·1	−16·7
47 10			48 55		
	+15·4	−16·9		+15·2	−16·6
50 46			52 44		
	+15·5	−16·8		+15·3	−16·5
54 49			57 02		
	+15·6	−16·7		+15·4	−16·4
59 23			61 51		
	+15·7	−16·6		+15·5	−16·3
64 30			67 17		
	+15·8	−16·5		+15·6	−16·2
70 12			73 16		
	+15·9	−16·4		+15·7	−16·1
76 26			79 43		
	+16·0	−16·3		+15·8	−16·0
83 05			86 32		
	+16·1	−16·2		+15·9	−15·9
90 00			90 00		

Note: App. Alt. = Apparent altitude = Sextant altitude corrected for index error and dip.

Figure 1–6. **Portion of the *Nautical Almanac*'s Altitude Correction Tables, showing an R-correction of +15.6′ to an observation of the sun's lower limb in June, at an apparent altitude of 69°43.2.′**

both a permanent record and a regular routine which reduces the chance of error. There are as many variations of workforms as there are navigators, and you will eventually find forms that suit you best. The Appendix contains blank workbook forms that I have found to be most useful, and all the practical examples in this book have been worked out on those forms. If we had been keeping one with the data we have accumulated until now, it would look like this:

DATE	June 8, 1984
BODY	Sun $\underline{\odot}$
hs	69-48.5
IC	-2.4
D	-2.9
ha	69-43.2
R	+15.6
Ho	69-58.8

The symbol $\underline{\odot}$ indicates that the observation was of the sun's lower limb, and you will see all the other pertinent values and algebraic totals which were entered as we went along. We will continue with the form as we move on to the next step, taking the time of the sight.

2 Timing the Sight

In navigating through coastal waters, timing a bearing to the nearest minute is usually good enough, because the vessel is moving relatively slowly, and the landmarks are fixed. In celestial observations, however, the bodies from which position lines are derived are constantly in motion with respect to the earth, and accurate positioning requires timing to the nearest *second*. In an exercise like your sun sight, for example, being 1 minute off in time could mean being up to 15 miles off in position.

Historically, the difficulty in obtaining accurate time was the navigator's nemesis, but the advent of electronic watches, and the availability of radio time signals anywhere in the world, make it an easy matter today. Time, in fact, has enjoyed the most rapid technological advance of any part of the navigational art. Clock time, actually a measure of the earth's rotation, was first reckoned in terms of celestial phenomena, then later by mechanical means, and today, with extraordinary precision, by using the vibrations of atoms as the regulator.

Although we still relate time to the sun's apparent movement, the development of accurate clocks showed that that movement, due to variations in the earth's rotation, is not uniform. As a consequence, a fictitious "mean sun" is imagined to be moving westward at a constant 15 degrees per hour, averaging out the irregularities so that we can measure time in a consistent manner. In our civil lives in North America, we divide that average 24-hour day into two 12-hour segments, A.M. (ante meridiem) and P.M. (post meridiem), to distinguish between events occurring before or after noon. In many parts of the world, and universally for navigational purposes, the 24-hour clock is used, and time is expressed as four digits, such at 0705 for 7:05 A.M., or 1645 for 4:45 P.M.

For convenience, most people like to think of the sun rising and setting at prescribed times wherever they are, but if a single, universal time were used, the phenomena would occur at different times in each location. So, a series of time zones was established, in which geographical regions adopted a common standard time more nearly representative of solar time in their area. Starting in 1883, with the adoption by the railroads of four time zones for the continental United States, the scheme is now used worldwide. The zones are generally established at 15° intervals (representing 1 hour's movement of the mean sun) centered at Greenwich, England, where 0° longitude was established by international agreement. Each time zone is identified by a "zone description" (ZD), which is expressed as the number of whole hours that must be applied to the local zone time to obtain the correct time at Greenwich. Figure 2–1 lists the 24 zones and their prescribed limits and zone descriptions. In some instances, boundaries may be arbitrarily adjusted to conform to local custom, or, as in the case of daylight saving time, an area may choose to keep the time of the adjacent zone to

Time Zones. Zone Descriptions, and Suffixes		
ZONE	ZD	SUFFIX
7½°W. to 7½°E.	0	Z
7½°E. to 22½°E.	− 1	A
22½°E. to 37½°E.	− 2	B
37½°E. to 52½°E.	− 3	C
52½°E. to 67½°E.	− 4	D
67½°E. to 82½°E.	− 5	E
82½°E. to 97½°E.	− 6	F
97½°E. to 112½°E.	− 7	G
112½°E. to 127½°E.	− 8	H
127½°E. to 142½°E.	− 9	I
142½°E. to 157½°E.	−10	K
157½°E. to 172½°E.	−11	L
172½°E. to 180°	−12	M
7½°W. to 22½°W.	+ 1	N
22½°W. to 37½°W.	+ 2	O
37½°W. to 52½°W.	+ 3	P
52½°W. to 67½°W.	+ 4	Q
67½°W. to 82½°W.	+ 5	R
82½°W. to 97½°W.	+ 6	S
97½°W. to 112½°W.	+ 7	T
112½°W. to 127½°W.	+ 8	U
127½°W. to 142½°W.	+ 9	V
142½°W. to 157½°W.	+10	W
157½°W. to 172½°W.	+11	X
172½°W. to 180°	+12	Y

Figure 2–1. **Time Zones and their Zone Descriptions from Bowditch, *American Practical Navigator*, Table 36.**

their east. The standard times kept in various places or countries are listed in the almanac.

It is normal practice at sea to set the ship's clocks to the time of the zone in which you are sailing, advancing or retarding them by an hour as you move from zone to zone. Thus, in Longitude 75°W, with a normal ZD of +5, 7 A.M. is the equivalent of noon in Greenwich. During the summer months, when daylight saving time is in effect, the ZD for the 75°W-zone advances to +4, so 0700 then is only 1100 in Greenwich.

As a convention, the time at Greenwich has been adopted as the universal time for celestial navigation. The almanac presents all of its astronomical data in terms of Greenwich mean time (GMT), although that can, of course, be converted to any local time by applying the zone description. Present-day technology has, to an extent, outstripped historical convention, and with the exceptional accuracy of atomic clocks, it has been discovered that time based on the mean sun is no longer exact. So, a new term, *coordinated universal time* (UTC), more closely tied to the earth's actual rotation, is used by technicians, and is the basis for the Bureau of Standards' radio time-broadcasts. UTC, as broadcast, may vary by a fraction of a second from Greenwich mean time as used in the almanac, but for practical purposes, celestial navigators can use the two times interchangeably.

Since the almanac data are presented in terms of Greenwich mean time, using the 24-hour clock, I find it easiest to set a digital watch to GMT, so that the exact time of a sight can be read out directly. Whenever possible, experienced navigators try to check a timepiece daily by radio time-ticks, and if it is a simple matter to reset it, the watch can always display the correct time. If you don't choose to keep Greenwich time on your watch, or if you don't wish to reset it, you can simply compare its reading with the correct time, make a note of the error, and apply the necessary correction when you record the time of your sight.

At sea, unless you are fortunate enough to have a fellow crewmember to read the time and record it for you, you have to time your sights yourself. I have found it handiest in that circumstance to move my watch to the inside of my left wrist, or to hold it in the palm of my left hand, and then, at the instant that the reflected image touches the horizon, I glance first at the watch time, and record it, and then read the sextant at my convenience.

Returning now to our practical example, let's assume that you have your watch time (W) set to GMT, and that a recent time-tick showed it to be right on the second; zero correction needed. Say, also, that you took your sight just before noon, local time, and your watch read, 15 hours, 56 minutes, 51 seconds. Adding this information to your workbook, the form to date would look like this:

DATE	June 8, 1984
BODY	Sun ☉
hs	69 – 48.5
IC	–2.4
D	–2.9
ha	69 – 43.2
R	+ 15.6
Ho	69 – 58.8
W	15-56-51
corr	00
GMT	15-56-51

With this GMT, 15–56–51, and the date, June 8, 1984, you are now ready to enter the almanac.

3 The Almanac

You have already been introduced to the *Nautical Almanac* when you used its altitude correction tables in Chapter 1. Now it is time to turn to its daily pages to establish the sun's precise position in the sky at the time of your sight. The almanac contains all the astronomical data a navigator needs to proceed with the solution of his sight, as well as a wealth of auxiliary and planning information, and an excellent explanatory section.

There are two choices of almanacs: the *Nautical Almanac*, which is published in a single volume for each calendar year; and the *American Air Almanac*, which is issued in semiannual editions. Both are prepared by the United States Naval Observatory and are published by the Government Printing Office. Although some years ago there was an argument for the simplicity and presentation of the *Air Almanac*, the *Nautical Almanac* has since adopted a straightforward, convenient format, and I prefer it, not only for the single-volume aspect, but also for its auxiliary information specifically oriented to the marine navigator. All the examples in this book have been computed with the use of the *Nautical Almanac.*

The two pieces of information you need from the almanac for your sun sight are the Greenwich hour angle (GHA) and declination (Dec) of the sun at the exact time of the observation. GHA and declination are the coordinates, corresponding to longitude and latitude on earth, of a body on the celestial sphere whose location we must pinpoint in order to derive a line of position. The celestial sphere? It doesn't actually exist; it is just an imaginary sphere, concentric with the earth and with the earth at its center, which provides a convenient matrix for locating celestial bodies, all of which are presumed to be projected on it, just as they are on the dome of a planetarium. The earth's rotation from west to east causes the apparent westward movement of the bodies on the celestial sphere—an easy way to conceptualize the relative motion between the earth and the heavenly bodies. The Greenwich hour angle is the angular distance measured westward from the meridian of Greenwich, 0°, as is West longitude. Declination, like latitude, is the angular distance north (or south) of the celestial equator. The relationship between the horizontal coordinates, GHA, longitude, and local hour angle (a measurement we will discuss later in this chapter), is illustrated in Figure 3–1.

Proceeding with the sun sight, the almanac is opened to the daily pages for June 8, where the astronomical data for all the navigational bodies are displayed for a 3-day period. We are presently interested in the right-hand page, or "sun side," a reproduction of which is shown in Figure 3–2. Notice that GHA and Dec are presented for each whole hour of Greenwich mean time. Figure 3–3 is an enlargement of the portion of the table applicable to your sun sight. If you look down the SUN column to the

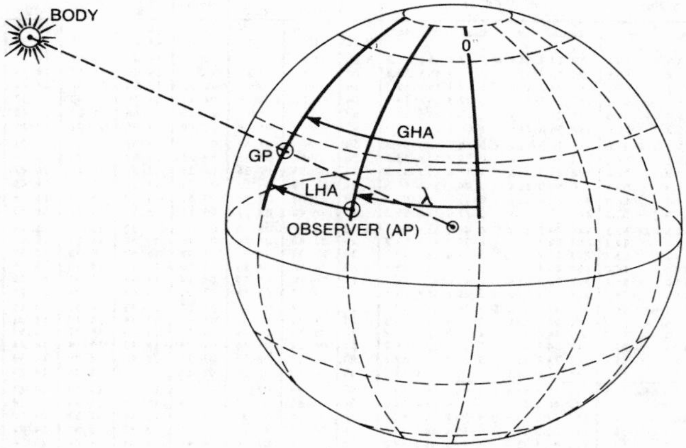

Figure 3–1. **The Relationship between Horizontal Coordinates. Greenwich hour angle, GHA, is measured westward from the Greenwich meridian, 0°, to the meridian of the celestial body; GP, geographical position, represents the point on Earth directly beneath the body. Longitude,λ, is measured West (or East) from Greenwich to the observer. Local hour angle, LHA, is measured West from the observer to the celestial body.**

hour of GMT at which the sight was taken (remember, in Chapter 2, that the Greenwich mean time was 15–56–51), you will see opposite 15^h a GHA of 45°14.1′, and a Dec of 22°54.0′ North. You have to adjust both of these values for the 56 minutes and 51 seconds of time remaining, and, in the case of the Greenwich hour angle, this is done by turning to the yellow *Increments and Corrections* tables in the back of the almanac. An excerpt of the table for 56 minutes is shown in Figure 3–4. Descending the SUN column, look opposite 51^s to find the sun's GHA increment of 14°12.8′. This is added to the tabular value for 15 hours from the daily page to produce the GHA for 15–56–51 of 59°26.9′.

G.M.T.		SUN G.H.A.	SUN Dec.	MOON G.H.A.	MOON v	MOON Dec.	MOON d	MOON H.P.
d	h	° ′	° ′	° ′	′	° ′	′	′
8	00	180 15.9	N22 50.6	70 23.2	11.5	N 2 23.8	15.5	59.3
	01	195 15.8	50.9	84 53.7	11.5	2 08.3	15.5	59.3
	02	210 15.7	51.1	99 24.2	11.5	1 52.8	15.5	59.3
	03	225 15.5	·· 51.3	113 54.7	11.6	1 37.3	15.6	59.3
	04	240 15.4	51.5	128 25.3	11.5	1 21.7	15.5	59.3
	05	255 15.3	51.8	142 55.8	11.5	1 06.2	15.5	59.3
	06	270 15.2	N22 52.0	157 26.3	11.6	N 0 50.7	15.5	59.3
	07	285 15.1	52.2	171 56.9	11.6	0 35.2	15.6	59.3
	08	300 14.9	52.4	186 27.5	11.5	0 19.6	15.5	59.3
F	09	315 14.8	·· 52.6	200 58.0	11.6	N 0 04.1	15.6	59.3
R	10	330 14.7	52.9	215 28.6	11.6	S 0 11.5	15.5	59.3
I	11	345 14.6	53.1	229 59.2	11.5	0 27.0	15.5	59.3
D	12	0 14.5	N22 53.3	244 29.7	11.6	S 0 42.5	15.5	59.3
A	13	15 14.3	53.5	259 00.3	11.6	0 58.0	15.6	59.3
Y	14	30 14.2	53.7	273 30.9	11.5	1 13.6	15.5	59.3
	15	45 14.1	·· 54.0	288 01.4	11.6	1 29.1	15.5	59.3
	16	60 14.0	54.2	302 32.0	11.5	1 44.6	15.5	59.3
	17	75 13.9	54.4	317 02.5	11.6	2 00.1	15.4	59.3
	18	90 13.7	N22 54.6	331 33.1	11.5	S 2 15.5	15.5	59.3
	19	105 13.6	54.8	346 03.6	11.6	2 31.0	15.5	59.3
	20	120 13.5	55.0	0 34.2	11.5	2 46.5	15.4	59.2
	21	135 13.4	·· 55.2	15 04.7	11.5	3 01.9	15.4	59.2
	22	150 13.3	55.4	29 35.2	11.5	3 17.3	15.4	59.2
	23	165 13.1	55.7	44 05.7	11.5	3 32.7	15.4	59.2
9	00	180 13.0	N22 55.9	58 36.2	11.4	S 3 48.1	15.3	59.2
	01	195 12.9	56.1	73 06.6	11.5	4 03.4	15.4	59.2
	02	210 12.8	56.3	87 37.1	11.4	4 18.8	15.3	59.2
	03	225 12.7	·· 56.5	102 07.5	11.4	4 34.1	15.2	59.2
	04	240 12.5	56.7	116 37.9	11.4	4 49.3	15.3	59.2
	05	255 12.4	56.9	131 08.3	11.4	5 04.6	15.2	59.2
	06	270 12.3	N22 57.1	145 38.7	11.4	S 5 19.8	15.2	59.2
	07	285 12.2	57.3	160 09.1	11.3	5 35.0	15.2	59.2
S	08	300 12.0	57.5	174 39.4	11.3	5 50.2	15.1	59.2
A	09	315 11.9	·· 57.7	189 09.7	11.3	6 05.3	15.1	59.2
T	10	330 11.8	57.9	203 40.0	11.3	6 20.4	15.1	59.2
U	11	345 11.7	58.1	218 10.3	11.2	6 35.5	15.0	59.1
R	12	0 11.6	N22 58.3	232 40.5	11.2	S 6 50.5	15.0	59.1
D	13	15 11.4	58.5	247 10.7	11.2	7 05.5	14.9	59.1
A	14	30 11.3	58.7	261 40.9	11.2	7 20.4	14.9	59.1
Y	15	45 11.2	·· 58.9	276 11.1	11.1	7 35.3	14.9	59.1
	16	60 11.1	59.1	290 41.2	11.1	7 50.2	14.8	59.1
	17	75 10.9	59.3	305 11.3	11.0	8 05.0	14.7	59.1
	18	90 10.8	N22 59.5	319 41.3	11.1	S 8 19.7	14.8	59.1
	19	105 10.7	59.7	334 11.4	11.0	8 34.5	14.6	59.1
	20	120 10.6	22 59.9	348 41.4	10.9	8 49.1	14.6	59.1
	21	135 10.4	23 00.1	3 11.3	10.9	9 03.7	14.6	59.1
	22	150 10.3	00.3	17 41.2	10.9	9 18.3	14.5	59.0
	23	165 10.2	00.5	32 11.1	10.9	9 32.8	14.5	59.0
10	00	180 10.1	N23 00.7	46 41.0	10.8	S 9 47.3	14.4	59.0
	01	195 10.0	00.9	61 10.8	10.8	10 01.7	14.3	59.0
	02	210 09.8	01.0	75 40.6	10.7	10 16.0	14.3	59.0
	03	225 09.7	·· 01.2	90 10.3	10.7	10 30.3	14.2	59.0
	04	240 09.6	01.4	104 40.0	10.6	10 44.5	14.2	59.0
	05	255 09.5	01.6	119 09.6	10.7	10 58.7	14.1	59.0
	06	270 09.3	N23 01.8	133 39.3	10.5	S11 12.8	14.0	59.0
	07	285 09.2	02.0	148 08.8	10.6	11 26.8	14.0	58.9
	08	300 09.1	02.2	162 38.4	10.4	11 40.8	13.9	58.9
S	09	315 09.0	·· 02.4	177 07.8	10.5	11 54.7	13.8	58.9
U	10	330 08.8	02.5	191 37.3	10.4	12 08.5	13.8	58.9
N	11	345 08.7	02.7	206 06.7	10.3	12 22.3	13.7	58.9
D	12	0 08.6	N23 02.9	220 36.0	10.3	S12 36.0	13.6	58.9
A	13	15 08.5	03.1	235 05.3	10.2	12 49.6	13.6	58.9
Y	14	30 08.3	03.3	249 34.5	10.3	13 03.2	13.4	58.9
	15	45 08.2	·· 03.5	264 03.8	10.1	13 16.6	13.4	58.8
	16	60 08.1	03.6	278 32.9	10.1	13 30.0	13.3	58.8
	17	75 08.0	03.8	293 02.0	10.1	13 43.3	13.3	58.8
	18	90 07.8	N23 04.0	307 31.1	10.0	S13 56.6	13.1	58.8
	19	105 07.7	04.2	322 00.1	9.9	14 09.7	13.1	58.8
	20	120 07.6	04.4	336 29.0	9.9	14 22.8	13.0	58.8
	21	135 07.5	·· 04.5	350 57.9	9.9	14 35.8	12.9	58.8
	22	150 07.3	04.7	5 26.8	9.8	14 48.7	12.8	58.7
	23	165 07.2	04.9	19 55.6	9.7	15 01.5	12.7	58.7
		S.D. 15.8	d 0.2	S.D. 16.2		16.1		16.0

Lat.	Twilight Naut.	Twilight Civil	Sunrise	Moonrise 8	Moonrise 9	Moonrise 10	Moonrise 11
°	h m	h m	h m	h m	h m	h m	h m
N 72	□	□	□	14 03	16 22	18 59	■
N 70	□	□	□	14 01	16 09	18 27	21 38
68	□	□	□	14 00	15 59	18 04	20 27
66	////	////	00 33	13 58	15 50	17 46	19 51
64	////	////	01 41	13 57	15 43	17 32	19 26
62	////	////	02 15	13 56	15 37	17 20	19 06
60	////	01 04	02 40	13 55	15 32	17 10	18 49
N 58	////	01 47	02 59	13 55	15 27	17 01	18 36
56	////	02 15	03 15	13 54	15 23	16 54	18 24
54	00 59	02 36	03 29	13 53	15 20	16 47	18 14
52	01 38	02 53	03 41	13 53	15 16	16 41	18 05
50	02 04	03 07	03 51	13 52	15 13	16 35	17 57
45	02 47	03 36	04 13	13 51	15 07	16 23	17 40
N 40	03 17	03 58	04 31	13 50	15 02	16 14	17 26
35	03 40	04 16	04 46	13 50	14 57	16 06	17 14
30	03 58	04 31	04 58	13 49	14 53	15 58	17 04
20	04 26	04 55	05 20	13 48	14 46	15 46	16 47
N 10	04 48	05 15	05 38	13 47	14 41	15 35	16 31
0	05 07	05 33	05 56	13 46	14 35	15 25	16 17
S 10	05 24	05 50	06 13	13 45	14 30	15 15	16 03
20	05 39	06 07	06 31	13 44	14 24	15 05	15 49
30	05 55	06 25	06 51	13 43	14 17	14 53	15 32
35	06 04	06 36	07 04	13 43	14 14	14 46	15 22
40	06 13	06 47	07 17	13 42	14 09	14 38	15 11
45	06 23	07 00	07 34	13 42	14 05	14 29	14 58
S 50	06 34	07 16	07 54	13 41	13 59	14 19	14 42
52	06 40	07 23	08 04	13 40	13 56	14 14	14 35
54	06 45	07 31	08 14	13 40	13 53	14 08	14 27
56	06 51	07 40	08 27	13 40	13 50	14 02	14 18
58	06 58	07 50	08 41	13 39	13 47	13 56	14 08
S 60	07 05	08 01	08 58	13 39	13 43	13 48	13 56

Lat.	Sunset	Twilight Civil	Twilight Naut.	Moonset 8	Moonset 9	Moonset 10	Moonset 11
°	h m	h m	h m	h m	h m	h m	h m
N 72	□	□	□	01 44	01 15	{00 42 / 23 51}	■
N 70	□	□	□	01 42	01 20	00 57	{00 25 / 23 04}
68	□	□	□	01 40	01 25	01 10	00 50
66	23 32	////	////	01 38	01 29	01 20	01 09
64	22 19	////	////	01 36	01 33	01 29	01 25
62	21 45	////	////	01 35	01 36	01 36	01 38
60	21 20	22 56	////	01 34	01 38	01 43	01 49
N 58	21 00	22 13	////	01 33	01 41	01 49	01 59
56	20 44	21 45	////	01 32	01 43	01 54	02 07
54	20 30	21 23	23 02	01 31	01 45	01 58	02 15
52	20 18	21 06	22 22	01 31	01 46	02 03	02 22
50	20 07	20 51	21 55	01 30	01 48	02 07	02 28
45	19 45	20 23	21 12	01 29	01 51	02 15	02 41
N 40	19 28	20 00	20 42	01 27	01 54	02 22	02 52
35	19 13	19 43	20 19	01 26	01 57	02 28	03 02
30	19 00	19 28	20 01	01 25	01 59	02 33	03 10
20	18 39	19 03	19 32	01 24	02 03	02 43	03 25
N 10	18 20	18 43	19 10	01 22	02 06	02 51	03 38
0	18 03	18 25	18 51	01 20	02 09	02 59	03 50
S 10	17 46	18 09	18 35	01 19	02 12	03 06	04 02
20	17 28	17 52	18 19	01 17	02 16	03 15	04 15
30	17 07	17 33	18 03	01 15	02 20	03 24	04 30
35	16 55	17 23	17 54	01 14	02 22	03 30	04 38
40	16 41	17 11	17 45	01 13	02 24	03 36	04 48
45	16 24	16 58	17 35	01 12	02 27	03 43	05 00
S 50	16 04	16 42	17 24	01 10	02 31	03 52	05 14
52	15 55	16 35	17 19	01 09	02 32	03 56	05 21
54	15 44	16 27	17 13	01 08	02 34	04 01	05 28
56	15 32	16 18	17 07	01 07	02 36	04 06	05 36
58	15 17	16 09	17 01	01 06	02 38	04 12	05 46
S 60	15 01	15 57	16 53	01 05	02 41	04 18	05 57

Day	SUN Eqn. of Time 00ʰ	SUN Eqn. of Time 12ʰ	SUN Mer. Pass.	MOON Mer. Pass. Upper	MOON Mer. Pass. Lower	Age	Phase
	m s	m s	h m	h m	h m	d	
8	01 04	00 58	11 59	19 58	07 33	09	○
9	00 52	00 46	11 59	20 47	08 22	10	
10	00 41	00 35	11 59	21 37	09 12	11	

Figure 3–2. **Typical daily page from the *Nautical Almanac* for sun and moon**

1984 JUNE 8,

G.M.T.		SUN		MOON				
d	h	G.H.A. ° ′	Dec. ° ′	G.H.A. ° ′	*v* ′	Dec. ° ′	*d* ′	H
8	00	180 15.9	N22 50.6	70 23.2	11.5	N 2 23.8	15.5	5'
	01	195 15.8	50.9	84 53.7	11.5	2 08.3	15.5	5'
	02	210 15.7	51.1	99 24.2	11.5	1 52.8	15.5	5'
	03	225 15.5	·· 51.3	113 54.7	11.6	1 37.3	15.6	5'
	04	240 15.4	51.5	128 25.3	11.5	1 21.7	15.5	5'
	05	255 15.3	51.8	142 55.8	11.5	1 06.2	15.5	5'
	06	270 15.2	N22 52.0	157 26.3	11.6	N 0 50.7	15.5	5'
	07	285 15.1	52.2	171 56.9	11.6	0 35.2	15.6	5'
	08	300 14.9	52.4	186 27.5	11.5	0 19.6	15.5	5'
F	09	315 14.8	·· 52.6	200 58.0	11.6	N 0 04.1	15.6	5'
R	10	330 14.7	52.9	215 28.6	11.6	S 0 11.5	15.5	5'
I	11	345 14.6	53.1	229 59.2	11.5	0 27.0	15.5	5'
D	12	0 14.5	N22 53.3	244 29.7	11.6	S 0 42.5	15.5	5'
A	13	15 14.3	53.5	259 00.3	11.6	0 58.0	15.6	5'
Y	14	30 14.2	53.7	273 30.9	11.5	1 13.6	15.5	5'
	15	45 14.1	·· 54.0	288 01.4	11.6	1 29.1	15.5	5'
	16	60 14.0	54.2	302 32.0	11.5	1 44.6	15.5	5'
	17	75 13.9	54.4	317 02.5	11.6	2 00.1	15.4	5'
	18	90 13.7	N22 54.6	331 33.1	11.5	S 2 15.5	15.5	5'
	19	105 13.6	54.8	346 03.6	11.6	2 31.0	15.5	5'
	20	120 13.5	55.0	0 34.2	11.5	2 46.5	15.4	5'
	21	135 13.4	·· 55.2	15 04.7	11.5	3 01.9	15.4	5'
	22	150 13.3	55.4	29 35.2	11.5	3 17.3	15.4	5'
	23	165 13.1	55.7	44 05.7	11.5	3 32.7	15.4	5'
9	00	180 13.0	N22 55.9	58 36.2	11.4	S 3 48.1	15.3	5'
	01	[illegible]	[illegible]	[illegible]	[illegible]	[illegible]	[illegible]	[illegible]

Figure 3–3. **Excerpt from the *Nautical Almanac* showing astronomical data for the sun on June 8, 1984. At 15h GMT, the sun's GHA is 45°14.1′. The Dec at 15h is N22°54.0′, and at 16h, N22°54.2′**

The adjustment for declination is even easier. By inspection of Figure 3–3, you can see that the declination of the sun on June 8 is increasing slowly, at a rate of 0.2′ per hour. Since the time of your sight was almost at 16 hours, a +0.2′ correction would apply, and the resulting declination would read, 22°54.2′ North. Although this arithmetical interpolation can be made easily by eye, you should be aware that while the declination in this particular example was both northerly and increasing, that is

56ᵐ INCREMENTS AND CORRECTIONS

56ᵐ	SUN PLANETS	ARIES	MOON	v or d	Corrⁿ	v or d	Corrⁿ	v or d	Corrⁿ
s	° ′	° ′	° ′	′	′	′	′	′	′
00	14 00·0	14 02·3	13 21·7	0·0	0·0	6·0	5·7	12·0	11·3
01	14 00·3	14 02·6	13 22·0	0·1	0·1	6·1	5·7	12·1	11·4
02	14 00·5	14 02·8	13 22·2	0·2	0·2	6·2	5·8	12·2	11·5
03	14 00·8	14 03·1	13 22·4	0·3	0·3	6·3	5·9	12·3	11·6
04	14 01·0	14 03·3	13 22·7	0·4	0·4	6·4	6·0	12·4	11·7
05	14 01·3	14 03·6	13 22·9	0·5	0·5	6·5	6·1	12·5	11·8
06	14 01·5	14 03·8	13 23·2	0·6	0·6	6·6	6·2	12·6	11·9
07	14 01·8	14 04·1	13 23·4	0·7	0·7	6·7	6·3	12·7	12·0
08	14 02·0	14 04·3	13 23·6	0·8	0·8	6·8	6·4	12·8	12·1
09	14 02·3	14 04·6	13 23·9	0·9	0·8	6·9	6·5	12·9	12·1
45	14 11·3	14 13·6	13 32·5	4·5	4·2	10·5	9·9	16·5	15·5
46	14 11·5	14 13·8	13 32·7	4·6	4·3	10·6	10·0	16·6	15·6
47	14 11·8	14 14·1	13 32·9	4·7	4·4	10·7	10·1	16·7	15·7
48	14 12·0	14 14·3	13 33·2	4·8	4·5	10·8	10·2	16·8	15·8
49	14 12·3	14 14·6	13 33·4	4·9	4·6	10·9	10·3	16·9	15·9
50	14 12·5	14 14·8	13 33·7	5·0	4·7	11·0	10·4	17·0	16·0
51	14 12·8	14 15·1	13 33·9	5·1	4·8	11·1	10·5	17·1	16·1
52	14 13·0	14 15·3	13 34·1	5·2	4·9	11·2	10·5	17·2	16·2
53	14 13·3	14 15·6	13 34·4	5·3	5·0	11·3	10·6	17·3	16·3
54	14 13·5	14 15·8	13 34·6	5·4	5·1	11·4	10·7	17·4	16·4
55	14 13·8	14 16·1	13 34·9	5·5	5·2	11·5	10·8	17·5	16·5
56	14 14·0	14 16·3	13 35·1	5·6	5·3	11·6	10·9	17·6	16·6
57	14 14·3	14 16·6	13 35·3	5·7	5·4	11·7	11·0	17·7	16·7
58	14 14·5	14 16·8	13 35·6	5·8	5·5	11·8	11·1	17·8	16·8
59	14 14·8	14 17·1	13 35·8	5·9	5·6	11·9	11·2	17·9	16·9
60	14 15·0	14 17·3	13 36·1	6·0	5·7	12·0	11·3	18·0	17·0

Figure 3–4. **Excerpt from the *Increments and Corrections* tables, showing an increment of 14°12.8′ to the sun's GHA for 56 minutes, 51 seconds of time**

not always the case, and one must be careful in applying a correction in the right direction. Because you are working with values obtained from a variety of sources, it is a good idea to enter each figure promptly in your workbook to avoid error. For our present exercise, the workform should now look like this:

DATE	June 8, 1984
BODY	Sun ☉
hs	69- 48.5
IC	-2.4
D	-2.9
ha	69 - 43.2
R	+15.6
Ho	69 -58.8
W	15-56-51
corr	00
GMT	15-56-51
gha	45 - 14.1
incr	14-12.8
GHA	59 -26.9
Dec	22-54.2N

Next, you must determine the sun's local hour angle (LHA) for your sight. LHA is the same sort of measurement as GHA, except that it originates at the observer's local meridian, not at the prime meridian at Greenwich (Figure 3–1). The determination is made by applying the observer's longitude to the Greenwich hour angle previously calculated. For convenience, a longitude is selected near your dead reckoning position, such that LHA will work out to a whole degree, thereby eliminating one interpolation in the sight reduction table. The selected longitude is called the assumed longitude, and is abbreviated $a\lambda$. Since the sun's apparent movement is toward the west, you will subtract the assumed longitude from the GHA if the longitude is West, and add the longitude to the GHA if the longitude is East. Figure 3–1 will help you understand this relationship, but it may be still easier just to remember the simple formula:

$$\text{LHA} = \text{GHA} \begin{array}{c} -\text{West} \\ +\text{East} \end{array} \text{Longitude}$$

For our practical example, let's arbitrarily establish your DR, or dead reckoning position, at the time of your sun sight at 40°43′N, 70°14′W. Since the GHA worked out to be 59°26.9′, a convenient assumed longitude nearby, one which would make the local hour angle come out to a whole degree, would be 70°26.9′W. Following the rule for applying the assumed longitude to the GHA, the 70°26.9′ should be subtracted from the GHA, but, as you will have already noticed, the GHA is smaller than the assumed longitude; what do we do? Checkmate? Not at all. This is just an example of the occasional case in which West longitude exceeds GHA; you simply add 360° to the Greenwich hour angle and proceed from there. Should you ever find yourself in East longitudes, and the sum of the GHA and the assumed longitude exceeds 360°, the correct LHA is found by subtracting 360° from the total. In our example, by adding 360° to GHA, and then subtracting the assumed longitude, the LHA works out to 349°. Entering this, and an assumed latitude, aL, of 41° N—the nearest whole degree to your DR latitude—your workbook should look like this:

DATE	June 8, 1984
BODY	Sun ☉̲
hs	69-48.5
IC	-2.4
D	-2.9
ha	69 - 43.2
R	+ 15.6
Ho	69 -58.8
W	15-56-51
corr	00
GMT	15-56-51
gha	45-14.1
incr	14 -12.8
GHA	59-26.9
	360
	419-26.9
aλ	-70-26.9
LHA	349
Dec	22-54.2 N
aL	41 N

You have now established both the coordinates of your assumed position, AP, which will be needed for the sixth and final step, plotting the line of position. In our exercise these are:

aL	41°N
aλ	70°26.9′W

You also have the three values needed to enter the sight reduction table, the next step in the celestial procedure.

LHA	349°
Dec	22°54.2′N
aL	41°N

4 Calculating the Computed Altitude

The fourth step in the six-step process of deriving a line of position from an observation of a celestial body is to calculate what the altitude of the body would have measured had you been exactly at the assumed position. That "computed altitude" (Hc) can then be compared with the altitude observed (Ho) to determine the observer's true location in relation to the assumed position. The calculation, which involves the solution of a spherical triangle, can be performed by the traditional methods of spherical trigonometry, but if the name doesn't frighten you the work required will. The mathematics were so burdensome, in fact, before the advent of electronic calculators, that for two centuries navigators devoted their efforts to the development of tables for simplifying the solution. As a result, inspection tables for sight reduction were born, and virtually all celestial navigators use them today, if not as their primary means, certainly as their ultimate backup. The solution by calculator is discussed in Chapter 12, but first you should become thoroughly familiar with the tabular method, the one we will use to complete our practice sight.

There are a number of sight reduction tables that have appeared over the years, and, like fishermen with their lures, each navigator has his favorite. Some continue to use the old table known as Dreisonstok (Pub. No. 208), which first appeared over fifty years ago and still finds its way into print from time to time, while others prefer Ageton (Pub. No. 211), because it is so compact. Many merchant mariners still use Pub. No. 214, which was the Navy standard during World War II and was the forerunner of the modern inspection tables, although it has now been superceded by Pub. No. 229, *Sight Reduction Tables for Marine Navigation,* and Pub. No. 249, *Sight Reduction Tables for Air Navigation*. Both of these latter tables are currently being published by the Defense Mapping Agency (DMA), and are available through DMA-authorized sales agents.

Which sight reduction table is for you? You have the choice between the completeness and precision of Pub. No. 229, or the speed and simplicity of Pub. No. 249. I recommend the latter to yachtsmen, because it is easier to learn, cheaper to buy, quicker to use, and its accuracy is entirely consistent with the accuracy that can be expected in observations made from a small boat at sea. In any case, once you learn how Pub. No. 249 works, it is not hard to learn the other table; they are quite similar in concept. Don't be misled by the "Air Navigation" in the title of Pub. No. 249; the tables are completely compatible with the *Nautical Almanac,* and have found widespread acceptance among marine navigators.

DMA Pub. No. 249 is issued in three volumes: Volume I is for selected stars, and is discussed in Chapter 9; Volume II, for latitudes 0°–39°, and Volume III, for latitudes 40°–89°, provide for the reduction of sights of the sun, moon, and planets, and for sights of stars whose declination is within the range 0°–29°. Volume I is updated every five years—we will be using Epoch 1985.0 for our examples—but Volumes II and III remain the same, and are simply reprinted from time to time.

For reducing our sun sight, we will need Volume III which covers our 41° assumed latitude. Open the table to the pages for 41° and select the one that covers the declination we calculated, 22°54.2′. Since both the declination and the assumed latitude were North, their name is the same, so we want the page entitled, "Lat.41° Declination (15°–29°) Same Name as Latitude." An illustration of the appropriate page, greatly reduced in size, is seen in Figure 4–1. To follow our practical exercise, an enlarged excerpt of a portion of this page is shown in Figure 4–2.

Descending the LHA column—in this case, at the right-hand side of the table—find the value of the local hour angle we had previously calculated: 349°. Then, in the column under the whole degree of declination, 22°, find, opposite LHA, the computed altitude, Hc; here, 68° 51′. Note this, along with the values for *d*, the tabulated difference per degree of declination, and Z, the azimuth angle, both of which we will come to in a moment. The computed altitude from the table, Tab Hc, was for the whole degree of declination, so it must now be adjusted to include the remaining 54.2′. This can be done by multiplying the tabular difference, *d*, from the table (+55′) by the incremental declination in fractional degrees (54.2/60), and applying the product, +49.7′, to the

Figure 4–1. Selected page from Volume III, Pub. No. 249, _Sight Reduction Tables for Air Navigation._ Much in favor with yachtsmen, Pub. No. 249 is the quickest and easiest to use of all sight reduction tables.

LAT 41°

LHA	15° Hc	15° d	15° Z	16° Hc	16° d	16° Z	17° Hc	17° d	17° Z	18° Hc	18° d	18° Z	19° Hc	19° d	19° Z
	° ′	′	°	° ′	′	°	° ′	′	°	° ′	′	°	° ′	′	°
0	64 00	+60	180	65 00	+60	180	66 00	+60	180	67 00	+60	180	68 00	+60	180
1	63 59	60	178	64 59	60	178	65 59	60	178	66 59	60	178	67 59	60	178
2	63 57	59	176	64 56	60	176	65 56	60	175	66 56	60	175	67 56	60	175
3	63 52	60	173	64 52	60	173	65 52	59	173	66 51	60	173	67 51	60	173
4	63 46	60	171	64 46	59	171	65 45	60	171	66 45	59	170	67 44	60	170
5	63 38	+60	169	64 38	+59	169	65 37	+59	168	66 36	+59	168	67 35	+59	168
6	63 29	59	167	64 28	59	167	65 27	59	166	66 26	59	166	67 25	58	165
7	63 18	59	165	64 17	58	164	65 15	59	164	66 14	58	163	67 12	58	163
8	63 05	59	163	64 04	58	162	65 02	58	162	66 00	58	161	66 58	57	160
9	62 51	58	161	63 49	58	160	64 47	57	159	65 44	58	159	66 42	57	158
10	62 35	+58	159	63 33	+57	158	64 30	+57	157	65 27	+57	157	66 24	+56	156
11	62 18	57	157	63 15	57	156	64 12	56	155	65 08	57	154	66 05	55	154
12	61 59	57	155	62 56	56	154	63 52	56	153	64 48	56	152	65 44	55	151
13	61 39	56	153	62 35	56	152	63 31	55	151	64 26	55	150	65 21	55	149
14	61 18	55	151	62 13	55	150	63 08	55	149	64 03	54	148	64 57	54	147
15	60 55	+55	149	61 50	+55	148	62 45	+54	147	63 39	+53	146	64 32	+54	145
16	60 31	55	147	61 26	53	146	62 19	54	145	63 13	53	144	64 06	52	143
17	60 06	54	146	61 00	53	145	61 53	53	144	62 46	52	143	63 38	52	142
18	59 40	53	144	60 33	53	143	61 26	52	142	62 18	52	141	63 10	51	140
19	59 13	52	142	60 05	52	141	60 57	52	140	61 49	51	139	62 40	50	138
20	58 45	+51	141	59 36	+52	140	60 28	+51	138	61 19	+50	137	62 09	+50	136
21	58 15	51	139	59 06	51	138	59 57	50	137	60 47	50	136	61 37	49	135
22	57 45	51	137	58 36	50	136	59 26	49	135	60 15	49	134	61 04	49	133
23	57 14	50	136	58 04	49	135	58 53	49	134	59 42	49	133	60 31	47	131
24	56 42	49	134	57 31	49	133	58 20	49	132	59 09	47	131	59 56	47	130
25	56 09	+49	133	56 58	+48	132	57 46	+48	131	58 34	+47	130	59 21	+47	128
26	55 35	49	132	56 24	48	130	57 12	47	129	57 59	46	128	58 45	46	127
27	55 01	48	130	55 49	47	129	56 36	47	128	57 23	46	127	58 09	45	126
28	54 26	47	129	55 13	47	128	56 00	46	127	56 46	46	125	57 32	44	124
29	53 51	46	128	54 37	47	126	55 24	45	125	56 09	45	124	56 54	44	123
30	53 14	+47	126	54 01	+45	125	54 46	+45	124	55 31	+45	123	56 16	+43	122
31	52 37	46	125	53 23	45	124	54 08	45	123	54 53	44	122	55 37	43	120
32	52 00	45	124	52 45	45	123	53 30	44	122	54 14	44	120	54 58	42	119
33	51 22	45	123	52 07	44	122	52 51	44	120	53 35	43	119	54 18	42	118
34	50 44	44	121	51 28	44	120	52 12	43	119	52 55	43	118	53 38	42	117
35	50 05	+44	120	50 49	+43	119	51 32	+43	118	52 15	+42	117	52 57	+42	116
36	49 26	43	119	50 09	43	118	50 52	43	117	51 35	41	116	52 16	41	115
37	48 46	43	118	49 29	43	117	50 12	42	116	50 54	41	115	51 35	41	114
38	48 06	43	117	48 49	42	116	49 31	41	115	50 12	41	114	50 53	41	113
39	47 25	43	116	48 08	42	115	48 50	41	114	49 31	40	113	50 11	40	112
40	46 44	+42	115	47 26	+42	114	48 08	+41	113	48 49	+40	112	49 29	+40	111
41	46 03	42	114	46 45	41	113	47 26	41	112	48 07	40	111	48 47	39	110
42	45 22	41	113	46 03	41	112	46 44	40	111	47 24	40	110	48 04	39	109
43	44 40	41	112	45 21	41	111	46 02	40	110	46 42	39	109	47 21	39	108
44	43 58	41	111	44 39	40	110	45 19	40	109	45 59	39	108	46 38	38	107
45	43 15	+41	110	43 56	+40	109	44 36	+39	108	45 15	+39	107	45 54	+38	106
46	42 33	40	109	43 13	40	108	43 53	39	107	44 32	39	106	45 11	38	105
47	41 50	40	109	42 30	40	108	43 10	39	107	43 49	38	106	44 27	38	104
48	41 07	40	108	41 47	39	107	42 26	39	106	43 05	38	105	43 43	38	104
49	40 24	39	107	41 03	39	106	41 42	39	105	42 21	38	104	42 59	37	103
50	39 40	+40	106	40 20	+39	105	40 59	+38	104	41 37	+38	103	42 15	+37	102
51	38 57	39	105	39 36	39	104	40 15	38	103	40 53	37	102	41 30	37	101
52	38 13	39	104	38 52	38	103	39 30	38	102	40 08	38	101	40 46	37	100
53	37 29	39	104	38 08	38	103	38 46	38	102	39 24	37	101	40 01	37	100
54	36 45	39	103	37 24	38	102	38 02	37	101	38 39	37	100	39 16	37	99
55	36 01	+38	102	36 39	+38	101	37 17	+38	100	37 55	+37	99	38 32	+36	98
56	35 16	39	101	35 55	38	100	36 33	37	99	37 10	37	98	37 47	36	97
57	34 32	38	101	35 10	38	100	35 48	37	99	36 25	37	98	37 02	36	97
58	33 47	38	100	34 25	38	99	35 03	37	98	35 40	37	97	36 17	36	96
59	33 03	38	99	33 41	37	98	34 18	37	97	34 55	37	96	35 32	36	95
60	32 18	+38	98	32 56	+37	97	33 33	+37	96	34 10	+37	96	34 47	+36	95
61	31 33	38	98	32 11	37	97	32 48	37	96	33 25	37	95	34 02	36	94
62	30 48	38	97	31 26	37	96	32 03	37	95	32 40	36	94	33 16	36	93
63	30 03	38	96	30 41	37	95	31 18	37	94	31 55	36	93	32 31	36	92
64	29 18	38	95	29 56	37	95	30 33	36	94	31 09	37	93	31 46	36	92
65	28 33	+37	95	29 10	+37	94	29 47	+37	93	30 24	+37	92	31 01	+36	91
66	27 48	37	94	28 25	37	93	29 02	37	92	29 39	36	91	30 15	36	90
67	27 03	37	93	27 40	37	93	28 17	37	92	28 54	36	91	29 30	36	90
68	26 17	38	93	26 55	37	92	27 32	36	91	28 08	37	90	28 45	36	89
69	25 32	37	92	26 09	37	91	26 46	37	90	27 23	36	89	27 59	36	89

LHA	20° Hc	20° d	20° Z	21° Hc	21° d	21° Z	22° Hc	22° d	22° Z	23° Hc	23° d	23° Z	24° Hc	24° d	24° Z
	° ′	′	°	° ′	′	°	° ′	′	°	° ′	′	°	° ′	′	°
0	69 00	+60	180	70 00	+60	180	71 00	+60	180	72 00	+60	180	73 00	+60	180
1	68 59	60	177	69 59	60	177	70 59	60	177	71 59	60	177	72 59	60	177
2	68 56	60	175	69 56	60	175	70 56	59	174	71 55	60	174	72 55	60	174
3	68 51	59	172	69 50	60	172	70 50	60	172	71 50	59	171	72 49	59	171
4	68 44	59	170	69 43	59	169	70 42	59	169	71 41	59	168	72 40	59	168
5	68 34	+59	167	69 33	+59	167	70 32	+59	166	71 31	+59	165	72 30	+58	165
6	68 23	59	165	69 22	58	164	70 20	58	163	71 18	59	163	72 17	57	162
7	68 10	58	162	69 08	58	161	70 06	58	161	71 04	57	160	72 01	57	159
8	67 55	58	160	68 53	57	159	69 50	57	158	70 47	57	157	71 44	56	156
9	67 39	57	157	68 36	56	156	69 32	57	156	70 29	56	155	71 25	55	153
10	67 20	+57	155	68 17	+56	154	69 13	+55	153	70 08	+55	152	71 03	+55	151
11	67 00	56	153	67 56	55	152	68 51	55	151	69 46	54	150	70 40	54	148
12	66 39	55	151	67 34	54	149	68 28	54	148	69 22	54	147	70 16	52	146
13	66 16	54	148	67 10	54	147	68 04	53	146	68 57	52	145	69 49	52	143
14	65 51	54	146	66 45	53	145	67 38	52	144	68 30	52	143	69 22	51	141
15	65 26	+52	144	66 18	+52	143	67 10	+52	142	68 02	+51	140	68 53	+50	139
16	64 58	52	142	65 50	52	141	66 42	50	140	67 32	50	138	68 22	49	137
17	64 30	51	140	65 21	51	139	66 12	50	138	67 02	49	136	67 51	48	135
18	64 01	50	139	64 51	50	137	65 41	49	136	66 30	48	135	67 18	48	133
19	63 30	50	137	64 20	49	135	65 09	48	134	65 57	48	133	66 45	46	131
20	62 59	+49	135	63 48	+48	134	64 36	+47	132	65 23	+47	131	66 10	+46	129
21	62 26	48	133	63 14	48	132	64 02	47	131	64 49	46	129	65 35	44	128
22	61 53	47	132	62 40	47	130	63 27	46	129	64 13	45	128	64 58	44	126
23	61 18	47	130	62 05	47	129	62 52	45	127	63 37	44	126	64 21	44	124
24	60 43	47	129	61 30	45	127	62 15	45	126	63 00	44	124	63 44	42	123
25	60 08	+45	127	60 53	+45	126	61 38	+44	124	62 22	+43	123	63 05	+42	122
26	59 31	45	126	60 16	45	124	61 01	43	123	61 44	42	122	62 26	42	120
27	58 54	45	124	59 39	43	123	60 22	43	122	61 05	42	120	61 47	41	119
28	58 16	44	123	59 00	44	122	59 44	42	120	60 26	41	119	61 07	40	117
29	57 38	44	122	58 22	42	120	59 04	42	119	59 46	41	118	60 27	39	116
30	56 59	+43	120	57 42	+42	119	58 24	+41	118	59 05	+41	116	59 46	+39	115
31	56 20	42	119	57 02	42	118	57 44	41	117	58 25	39	115	59 04	39	114
32	55 40	42	118	56 22	41	117	57 03	41	115	57 44	39	114	58 23	38	113
33	55 00	42	117	55 42	40	116	56 22	40	114	57 02	39	113	57 41	38	112
34	54 20	41	116	55 01	40	114	55 41	39	113	56 20	39	112	56 59	37	110
35	53 39	+40	115	54 19	+40	113	54 59	+39	112	55 38	+38	111	56 16	+37	109
36	52 57	40	114	53 37	40	112	54 17	38	111	54 55	38	110	55 33	37	108
37	52 16	39	113	52 55	39	111	53 34	39	110	54 13	37	109	54 50	36	107
38	51 34	39	112	52 13	39	110	52 52	38	109	53 30	37	108	54 07	36	106
39	50 51	39	111	51 30	39	109	52 09	37	108	52 46	37	107	53 23	36	105
40	50 09	+39	110	50 48	+38	108	51 26	+37	107	52 03	+36	106	52 39	+36	105
41	49 26	38	109	50 04	38	107	50 42	37	106	51 19	36	105	51 55	36	104
42	48 43	38	108	49 21	38	107	49 59	36	105	50 35	36	104	51 11	35	103
43	48 00	38	107	48 38	37	106	49 15	36	104	49 51	36	103	50 27	35	102
44	47 16	38	106	47 54	37	105	48 31	36	104	49 07	36	102	49 43	34	101
45	46 32	+38	105	47 10	+37	104	47 47	+36	103	48 23	+35	102	48 58	+35	100
46	45 49	37	104	46 26	37	103	47 03	35	102	47 38	36	101	48 14	34	99
47	45 05	37	103	45 42	36	102	46 18	36	101	46 54	35	100	47 29	34	99
48	44 21	36	103	44 57	37	101	45 34	35	100	46 09	35	99	46 44	34	98
49	43 36	37	102	44 13	36	101	44 49	35	99	45 24	35	98	45 59	34	97
50	42 52	+36	101	43 28	+36	100	44 04	+36	99	44 40	+34	98	45 14	+34	96
51	42 07	37	100	42 44	36	99	43 20	35	98	43 55	34	97	44 29	34	96
52	41 23	36	99	41 59	36	98	42 35	35	97	43 10	34	96	43 44	34	95
53	40 38	36	99	41 14	36	98	41 50	35	96	42 25	34	95	42 59	34	94
54	39 53	36	98	40 29	36	97	41 05	35	96	41 40	34	95	42 14	33	94
55	39 08	+36	97	39 44	+36	96	40 20	+34	95	40 54	+35	94	41 29	+33	93
56	38 23	36	96	38 59	35	95	39 34	35	94	40 09	34	93	40 43	34	92
57	37 38	36	96	38 14	35	95	38 49	35	94	39 24	34	93	39 58	34	92
58	36 53	36	95	37 29	35	94	38 04	35	93	38 39	34	92	39 13	33	91
59	36 08	36	94	36 44	35	93	37 19	34	92	37 53	35	91	38 28	33	90
60	35 23	+35	94	35 58	+36	93	36 34	+34	92	37 08	+34	91	37 42	+34	90
61	34 38	35	93	35 13	35	92	35 48	35	91	36 23	34	90	36 57	34	89
62	33 52	36	92	34 28	35	91	35 03	35	90	35 38	34	89	36 12	33	88
63	33 07	36	92	33 43	35	91	34 18	34	90	34 52	34	89	35 26	34	88
64	32 22	35	91	32 57	35	90	33 32	35	89	34 07	34	88	34 41	34	87
65	31 37	+35	90	32 12	+35	89	32 47	+35	88	33 22	+34	87	33 56	+34	86
66	30 51	36	90	31 27	35	89	32 02	35	88	32 37	34	87	33 11	34	86
67	30 06	36	89	30 42	35	88	31 17	34	87	31 51	35	86	32 26	34	85
68	29 21	35	88	29 56	35	87	30 31	35	86	31 06	35	85	31 41	34	84
69	28 35	36	88	29 11	35	87	29 46	35	86	30 21	35	85	30 56	34	84

LHA	25° Hc	25° d	25° Z	26° Hc	26° d	26° Z	27° Hc	27° d	27° Z	28° Hc	28° d	28° Z	29° Hc	29° d	29° Z	LHA
	° ′	′	°	° ′	′	°	° ′	′	°	° ′	′	°	° ′	′	°	
0	74 00	+60	180	75 00	+60	180	76 00	+60	180	77 00	+60	180	78 00	+60	180	360
1	73 59	60	177	74 59	60	177	75 59	59	176	76 58	60	176	77 58	60	176	359
2	73 55	60	173	74 55	59	173	75 54	60	173	76 54	59	172	77 53	60	172	358
3	73 48	60	170	74 48	59	170	75 47	59	169	76 46	59	168	77 45	59	168	357
4	73 39	59	167	74 38	59	166	75 37	59	166	76 36	58	165	77 34	58	164	356
5	73 28	+58	164	74 26	+58	163	75 24	+58	162	76 22	+58	161	77 20	+57	160	355
6	73 14	58	161	74 12	57	160	75 09	57	159	76 06	57	157	77 03	55	156	354
7	72 58	57	158	73 55	57	157	74 52	55	155	75 47	56	154	76 43	54	152	353
8	72 40	56	155	73 36	56	154	74 32	54	152	75 26	55	151	76 21	53	149	352
9	72 20	55	152	73 15	55	151	74 10	53	149	75 03	53	148	75 56	52	146	351
10	71 58	+54	149	72 52	+53	148	73 45	+53	146	74 38	+52	145	75 30	+50	143	350
11	71 34	53	147	72 27	52	145	73 19	52	144	74 11	50	142	75 01	49	140	349
12	71 08	53	144	72 01	51	143	72 52	50	141	73 42	49	139	74 31	48	137	348
13	70 41	51	142	71 32	51	140	72 23	49	139	73 12	48	137	74 00	46	135	347
14	70 13	50	140	71 03	49	138	71 52	48	136	72 40	47	134	73 27	45	132	346
15	69 43	+49	137	70 32	+48	136	71 20	+47	134	72 07	+45	132	72 52	+45	130	345
16	69 11	49	135	70 00	47	134	70 47	46	132	71 33	44	130	72 17	43	128	344
17	68 39	47	133	69 26	46	132	70 12	45	130	70 57	44	128	71 41	42	126	343
18	68 06	46	131	68 52	45	130	69 37	44	128	70 21	42	126	71 03	41	124	342
19	67 31	46	130	68 17	44	128	69 01	43	126	69 44	41	124	70 25	40	122	341
20	66 56	+44	128	67 40	+44	126	68 24	+42	124	69 06	+41	122	69 47	+39	120	340
21	66 19	44	126	67 03	43	124	67 46	41	123	68 27	40	121	69 07	38	118	339
22	65 42	44	124	66 26	41	123	67 07	41	121	67 48	39	119	68 27	37	117	338
23	65 05	42	123	65 47	41	121	66 28	40	119	67 08	38	117	67 46	37	115	337
24	64 26	42	121	65 08	40	120	65 48	39	118	66 27	38	116	67 05	36	114	336
25	63 47	+41	120	64 28	+40	118	65 08	+39	116	65 47	+37	115	66 24	+35	113	335
26	63 08	40	119	63 48	39	117	64 27	38	115	65 05	37	113	65 42	34	111	334
27	62 28	40	117	63 08	38	116	63 46	37	114	64 23	36	112	64 59	35	110	333
28	61 47	39	116	62 26	38	114	63 04	37	113	63 41	36	111	64 17	33	109	332
29	61 06	39	115	61 45	37	113	62 22	37	111	62 59	35	110	63 34	33	108	331
30	60 25	+38	113	61 03	+37	112	61 40	+36	110	62 16	+34	109	62 50	+33	107	330
31	59 43	38	112	60 21	36	111	60 57	36	109	61 33	34	107	62 07	32	106	329
32	59 01	37	111	59 38	36	110	60 14	35	108	60 49	34	106	61 23	32	105	328
33	58 19	37	110	58 56	35	109	59 31	35	107	60 06	33	105	60 39	32	104	327
34	57 36	36	109	58 12	36	108	58 48	34	106	59 22	33	104	59 55	32	103	326
35	56 53	+36	108	57 29	+35	106	58 04	+34	105	58 38	+33	103	59 11	+31	102	325
36	56 10	36	107	56 46	34	106	57 20	34	104	57 54	32	102	58 26	32	101	324
37	55 26	36	106	56 02	34	105	56 36	34	103	57 10	32	102	57 42	31	100	323
38	54 43	35	105	55 18	34	104	55 52	33	102	56 25	32	101	56 57	31	99	322
39	53 59	35	104	54 34	34	103	55 08	33	101	55 41	31	100	56 12	31	98	321
40	53 15	+35	103	53 50	+33	102	54 23	+33	100	54 56	+32	99	55 28	+30	98	320
41	52 31	34	102	53 05	34	101	53 39	32	100	54 11	32	98	54 43	30	97	319
42	51 46	35	102	52 21	33	100	52 54	32	99	53 26	32	97	53 58	30	96	318
43	51 02	34	101	51 36	33	99	52 09	32	98	52 41	32	97	53 13	30	95	317
44	50 17	34	100	50 51	33	99	51 24	32	97	51 56	31	96	52 27	30	94	316
45	49 33	+33	99	50 06	+33	98	50 39	+32	96	51 11	+31	95	51 42	+30	94	315
46	48 48	34	98	49 22	32	97	49 54	32	96	50 26	31	94	50 57	30	93	314
47	48 03	34	97	48 37	32	96	49 09	32	95	49 41	31	94	50 12	30	92	313
48	47 18	34	97	47 52	32	95	48 24	32	94	48 56	31	93	49 27	29	92	312
49	46 33	33	96	47 06	33	95	47 39	32	94	48 11	30	92	48 41	30	91	311
50	45 48	+33	95	46 21	+33	94	46 54	+31	93	47 25	+31	92	47 56	+30	90	310
51	45 03	33	95	45 36	32	93	46 08	32	92	46 40	31	91	47 11	30	90	309
52	44 18	33	94	44 51	32	93	45 23	32	91	45 55	30	90	46 25	30	89	308
53	43 33	33	93	44 06	32	92	44 38	31	91	45 09	31	90	45 40	30	88	307
54	42 47	33	92	43 20	33	91	43 53	31	90	44 24	31	89	44 55	30	88	306
55	42 02	+33	92	42 35	+32	91	43 07	+32	89	43 39	+31	88	44 10	+30	87	305
56	41 17	33	91	41 50	32	90	42 22	32	89	42 54	30	88	43 24	31	86	304
57	40 32	33	90	41 05	32	89	41 37	31	88	42 08	31	87	42 39	30	86	303
58	39 46	33	90	40 19	33	89	40 52	31	88	41 23	31	86	41 54	30	85	302
59	39 01	33	89	39 34	32	88	40 06	32	87	40 38	31	86	41 09	30	85	301
60	38 16	+33	88	38 49	+32	87	39 21	+32	86	39 53	+31	85	40 24	+30	84	300
61	37 31	33	88	38 04	32	87	38 36	32	86	39 08	31	85	39 39	31	84	299
62	36 45	33	87	37 18	33	86	37 51	32	85	38 23	31	84	38 54	31	83	298
63	36 00	33	87	36 33	33	86	37 06	32	84	37 38	31	83	38 09	31	82	297
64	35 15	33	86	35 48	33	85	36 21	32	84	36 53	31	83	37 24	31	82	296
65	34 30	+33	85	35 03	+33	84	35 36	+32	83	36 08	+31	82	36 39	+32	81	295
66	33 45	33	85	34 18	33	84	34 51	32	83	35 23	32	82	35 55	31	81	294
67	33 00	33	84	33 33	33	83	34 06	32	82	34 38	32	81	35 10	31	80	293
68	32 15	33	84	32 48	33	83	33 21	33	82	33 54	32	81	34 26	31	80	292
69	31 30	33	83	32 03	33	82	32 36	31	81	33 09	32	80	33 41	32	79	291

S. Lat. {LHA greater than 180°........Zn=180−Z; LHA less than 180°........Zn=180+Z}

DECLINATION (15°-29°) SAME NAME AS LATITUDE

LAT 41°

N. Lat. {LHA greater than 180°.......... Zn=Z
{LHA less than 180°.......... Zn=360−Z

LAT 41° DECLINATION (15°-29°) SAME NAME AS LATITUDE

	15°			16°			17°			18°			19°			20°			21°			22°					
LHA	Hc	d	Z	Hc	d	Z	Hc	d	Z	Hc	d	Z	Hc	d	Z	Hc	d	Z	Hc	d	Z	Hc	d	Z	Hc	Z	LHA
	° ′	′	°	° ′	′	°	° ′	′	°	° ′	′	°	° ′	′	°	° ′	′	°	° ′	′	°	° ′	′	°	°	°	
0	64 00	+60	180	65 00	+60	180	66 00	+60	180	67 00	+60	180	68 00	+60	180	69 00	+60	180	70 00	+60	180	71 00	+60	180	72	180	360
1	63 59	60	178	64 59	60	178	65 59	60	178	66 59	60	178	67 59	60	178	68 59	60	177	69 59	60	177	70 59	60	177	71	176	359
2	63 57	59	176	64 56	60	176	65 56	60	175	66 56	60	175	67 56	60	175	68 56	60	175	69 56	60	175	70 56	59	174	71	172	358
3	63 52	60	173	64 52	60	173	65 52	59	173	66 51	60	173	67 51	60	173	68 51	59	172	69 50	60	172	70 50	60	172	71 5	168	357
4	63 46	60	171	64 46	59	171	65 45	60	171	66 45	59	170	67 44	60	170	68 44	59	170	69 43	59	169	70 42	59	169	71 41	164	356
5	63 38	+60	169	64 38	+59	169	65 37	+59	168	66 36	+59	168	67 35	+59	168	68 34	+59	167	69 33	+59	167	70 32	+59	166	71 31	50	355
6	63 29	59	167	64 28	59	167	65 27	59	166	66 26	59	166	67 25	58	165	68 23	59	165	69 22	58	164	70 20	58	163	71 18	6	354
7	63 18	59	165	64 17	58	164	65 15	59	164	66 14	58	163	67 12	58	163	68 10	58	162	69 08	58	161	70 06	58	161	71 04	52	353
8	63 05	59	163	64 04	58	162	65 02	58	162	66 00	58	161	66 58	57	160	67 55	58	160	68 53	57	159	69 50	57	158	70 47	149	352
9	62 51	58	161	63 49	58	160	64 47	57	159	65 44	58	159	66 42	57	158	67 39	57	157	68 36	56	156	69 32	57	156	70 2′	146	351
10	62 35	+58	159	63 33	+57	158	64 30	+57	157	65 27	+57	157	66 24	+56	156	67 20	+57	155	68 17	+56	154	69 13	+55	153	70 C	143	350
11	62 18	57	157	63 15	57	156	64 12	56	155	65 08	57	154	66 05	55	154	67 00	56	153	67 56	55	152	68 51	55	151	69 4	140	349
12	61 59	57	155	62 56	56	154	63 52	56	153	64 48	56	152	65 44	55	151	66 39	55	151	67 34	54	149	68 28	54	148	69 2.	137	348
13	61 39	56	153	62 35	56	152	63 31	55	151	64 26	55	150	65 21	55	149	66 1[illegible]	[illegible]	148	67 10	54	147	68 04	[illegible]	[illegible]	68 5[illegible]	135	[illegible]
14	61 18	55	151	[illegible]	55	150	63 08	[illegible]	[illegible]	[illegible]	[illegible]	148	64 57	[illegible]	[illegible]	[illegible]	[illegible]	[illegible]	[illegible]	[illegible]	[illegible]						

Figure 4–2. **Excerpt from Pub. No. 249, Volume III, showing the values for Latitude 41°N, Declination 22°N, and LHA 349° to be: Hc 68°51′, *d*+55′, Z 151°**

tabluar Hc. Even easier, use Table 5, *Correction to Tabulated Altitude for Minutes of Declination,* which is found at the back of the sight reduction tables. Figure 4–3 shows a portion of Table 5 by which we can figure the altitude adjustment.

Enter the heading of Table 5 with the value of *d* from the main table: here, +55′. Descend the vertical column to the entry opposite the minutes of declination: in our example, 54 is the nearest whole minute. The correction (+50′) is then applied to the tabular Hc of 68°51′, resulting in a computed altitude—the altitude as it would have been measured at the assumed position—of 69°41′. In our example, the value of *d* was positive as indicated by the + sign in the main table, but if the value is negative, it will be so designated. Always be careful to observe the proper sign in applying the correction to the tabular Hc.

TABLE 5.—Correction to Tabulated Altitude for Minutes of Declination

0	31	32	33	34	35	36	37	38	39	40	41	42	43	44	45	46	47	48	49	50	51	52	53	54	55	56	57	58	59	60	d / ′
0	0	0	0	0	0	0	0	0	0	0	0	0	0	0	0	0	0	0	0	0	0	0	0	0	0	0	0	0	0	0	0
0	1	1	1	1	1	1	1	1	1	1	1	1	1	1	1	1	1	1	1	1	1	1	1	1	1	1	1	1	1	1	1
1	1	1	1	1	1	1	1	1	1	1	1	1	1	1	2	2	2	2	2	2	2	2	2	2	2	2	2	2	2	2	2
2	2	2	2	2	2	2	2	2	2	2	2	2	2	2	2	2	2	2	2	2	3	3	3	3	3	3	3	3	3	3	3
2	2	2	2	2	2	2	2	3	3	3	3	3	3	3	3	3	3	3	3	3	3	3	4	4	4	4	4	4	4	4	4
[illegible]	3	3	[illegible]	[illegible]					[illegible]	3	3	4	4	4	[illegible]																
[illegible]	[illegible]	[illegible]	[illegible]	27	28	29	30	30	[illegible]						[illegible]	37	38	38	39	40	41	42	[illegible]	[illegible]	[illegible]	45	46	46	[illegible]	[illegible]	48
24	25	26	27	28	29	29	30	31	32	33	33	34	35	36	37	38	38	39	40	41	42	42	43	44	45	46	47	47	48	49	49
25	26	27	28	28	29	30	31	32	32	33	34	35	36	37	38	38	39	40	41	42	42	43	44	45	46	47	48	48	49	50	50
26	26	27	28	29	30	31	31	32	33	34	35	36	37	37	38	39	40	41	42	42	43	44	45	46	47	48	48	49	50	51	51
26	27	28	29	29	30	31	32	33	34	35	36	36	37	38	39	40	41	42	42	43	44	45	46	47	48	49	49	50	51	52	52
26	27	28	29	30	31	32	33	34	34	35	36	37	38	39	40	41	42	42	43	44	45	46	47	48	49	49	50	51	52	53	53
27	28	29	30	31	32	32	33	34	35	36	37	38	39	40	40	41	42	43	44	45	46	47	48	49	50	50	51	52	53	54	54
28	28	29	30	31	32	33	34	35	36	37	38	38	39	40	41	42	43	44	45	46	47	48	49	50	50	51	52	53	54	55	55
28	29	30	31	32	33	34	35	35	36	37	38	39	40	41	42	43	44	45	46	47	48	49	49	50	51	52	53	54	55	56	56
28	29	30	31	32	33	34	35	36	37	38	39	40	41	42	43	44	45	46	47	48	48	49	50	51	52	53	54	55	56	57	57
29	30	31	32	33	34	35	36	37	38	39	40	41	42	43	44	44	45	46	47	48	49	50	51	52	53	54	55	56	57	58	58
30	30	31	32	33	34	35	36	37	38	39	40	41	42	43	44	45	46	47	48	49	50	51	52	53	54	55	56	57	58	59	59

Figure 4–3. **Excerpt from Table 5, Pub. No. 249, showing a correction of 50′ for *d* of 55′ and incremental minutes of declination, 54**

Your workbook, with the additional entries from the sight reduction table, is now almost complete and should look like this:

DATE	June 8, 1984
BODY	Sun ☉
hs	69-48.5
IC	-2.4
D	- 2.9
ha	69-43.2
R	+15.6
Ho	69-58.8
W	15-56-51
corr	00
GMT	15-56-51
gha	45-14.1
incr	14-12.8
GHA	59-26.9
	360
	419-26.9
aλ	-70-26.9
LHA	349
Dec	22-54.2 N
aL	41 N
Tab. Hc	68-51
corr	+50
Hc	69-41.0

You will recall that earlier you noted Z in the main table to be 151°. Following the rules shown in the corner of the table, you can see that in North latitude, when the LHA is greater than 180°, Zn, which is the abbreviation for azimuth, or true bearing, is equal to Z. Since our sun sight was taken in North latitude, and since the local hour angle was 349°, or greater than 180°, the true bearing of the sun from the assumed position was 151°. We will carry this forward to the next step in which we establish the final values for plotting the line of position.

Zn	151°

5 Altitude Difference and Azimuth

Step five is very brief, consisting of determining the difference between the computed altitude, Hc, which you have just found from the sight reduction table, and the observed altitude, Ho, which you had worked out in Chapter 1. The difference between Hc and Ho is called the altitude difference or intercept and is abbreviated, a. In the case of our sun sight, the difference between our Hc of 69°41.0′ and our Ho of 69°58.8′ is 17.8′.

For our plot we will need to recognize which of the altitudes we compared was the larger. This will tell us whether our intercept will be drawn from our assumed position in the direction of the azimuth—"toward"—or on the reciprocal bearing—"away." The rule states: Ho greater, toward; Hc greater, away. Since, in our example, the observed altitude was the greater, the intercept will be plotted toward the azimuth direction. There are two mnemonics that sailors use to remember the rule. "Hogtied" (Ho greater, toward) and "Coast Guard Academy" (C greater, away).

As you make the intercept calculation and establish whether it is toward (T), or away (A), you will have completed your workbook for the sight, which in its final form, looks like this:

DATE	June 8, 1984
BODY	Sun ☉
hs	69-48.5
IC	-2.4
D	-2.9
ha	69-43.2
R	+15.6
Ho	69-58.8
W	15-56-51
corr	00
GMT	15-56-51
gha	45-14.1
incr	14-12.8
GHA	59-26.9
	360
	419-26.9
aλ	-70-26.9
LHA	349
Dec	22-54.2 N
aL	41 N
Tab. Hc	68-51
corr	+50
Hc	69-41.0
Ho	69-58.8
a	17.8 T
Zn	151°

For the purposes of review, let me restate our practical exercise in textbook terms so that you can retrace the five numerical steps in the completed workform. It is important that you can do this, because in future chapters, when we explore sights of the moon, planets, and stars, we will be emphasizing the small procedural differences, assuming that you are familiar with the basic process that we have now covered.

A navigator in DR position Latitude 40°43′N, Longitude 70°14′W, makes an observation of the sun's lower limb at 15:56:51, Greenwich mean time, on June 8, 1984. The sextant altitude reads 69°48.5′, and the sextant has an index correction of –2.4′. The height of eye is 9 feet. Find the intercept (a), whether it is toward (T) or away (A), and the true azimuth (Zn).
(Answer: a = 17.8′T; Zn = 151°; Plot from AP 41°N, 70°26.9′W)

With the intercept and azimuth in hand, we are now ready to turn to the plot to construct the line of position which we have derived from the observation of the sun.

6 Plotting the Line of Position

The sixth and final step in the celestial procedure is to plot the line of position resulting from your sextant observation and subsequent calculations. Figure 6–1 illustrates the method as it applies to our sun sight. The ship's track, properly labeled with the course and speed, has been entered earlier on the plot, and the dead reckoning position advanced to local noon. Since the actual observation was made three minutes before noon, it wasn't necessary to establish a separate DR since the vessel had only moved about 800 yards during the interval.

Using your workbook to supply the necessary data, you first locate and label the assumed position, AP. Because we had selected a whole degree of latitude, it is an easy matter to pinpoint the assumed position right on the latitude line at the appropriate longitude; ours, you will recall, was 70°26.9′W. Next, the intercept you calculated, 17.8′, is set on your dividers—a minute measured

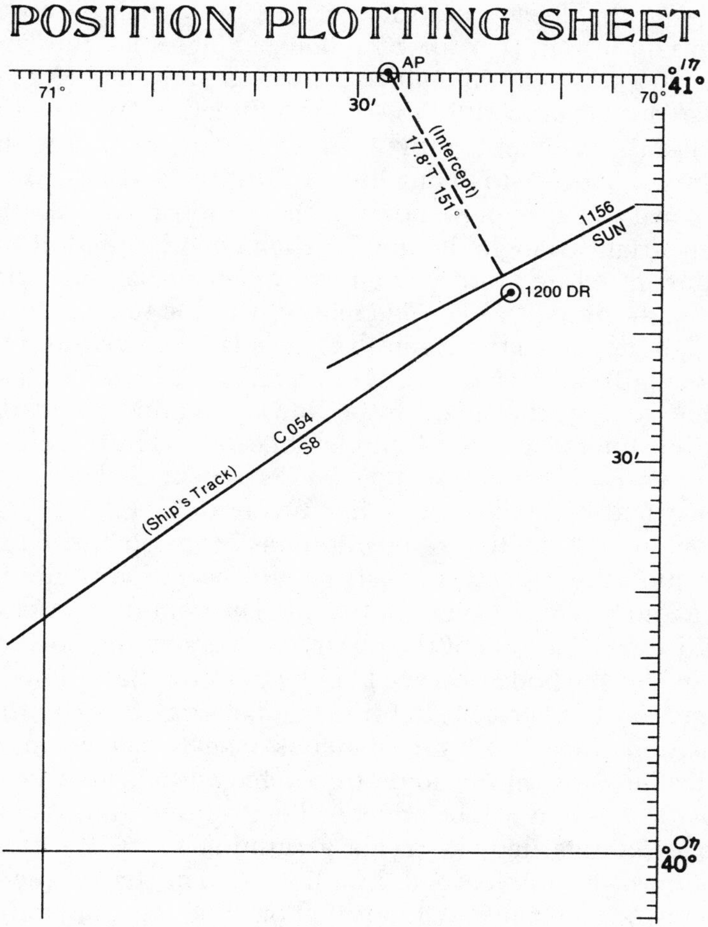

Figure 6–1. **Plotting the line of position from a sextant observation. The intercept is stepped off from the assumed position toward (or away from, when called for) the direction of the true azimuth. A perpendicular line is constructed at the end of the intercept; this is the line of position.**

on the adjacent latitude scale is equivalent to a nautical mile on the chart—and the distance is stepped off along the azimuth line. Your workbook shows that the true azimuth was 151°, and since Ho was greater than Hc, the intercept is stepped off *toward* the direction 151°. At the end of the intercept, a line is drawn perpendicular to the azimuth, and that is your line of position. A simple way to construct this perpendicular is by means of a draftsman's right triangle, laying the triangle at the end of the intercept while holding your protractor or parallel rules along the azimuth line. The reason why the line is drawn at right angles to the azimuth is because the position line is actually part of the circumference of a huge circle, a circle so large that a tangential line at the point where the radius intersects the circumference is virtually coincident with the circumference, and is a great deal easier to construct. We will discuss this further in Chapter 11.

Now that the line of position has been established on the plot, the necessary labels should be added promptly to avoid any chance of confusion. The common practice is to show the time of the observation above the position line, and the body observed below it, as has been done in Figure 6–1. Your celestial line can be crossed with other position lines from simultaneous visual, electronic, or celestial observations to produce a fix, and, like any other position line, it can be advanced or "retired" (navigator's lingo for retarded) to create a running fix in the same manner as you learned in piloting. The technique is reviewed in Chapter 13, but it should be remembered in establishing any fix, and especially one where celestial lines are used, that it is good practice not to rely on position lines which intersect at less than 30 degrees, unless no better lines are available.

Whether to use a plotting sheet or a chart for your plot is largely a matter of personal preference. When I am well offshore, I prefer a plotting sheet like the 960 series (formerly 3000–Z) published by the Defense Mapping Agency and illustrated in Figure 6–1. These plotting sheets use a Mercator projection like most nautical charts, have a scale of 4 inches to 1 degree of longitude, and are of a convenient dimension (17 × 22 inches) for the average yacht navigation station. You can, of course, use a chart equally well, provided the scale is not too small, and I find this particularly useful when I am nearing land and may have the opportunity to cross my celestial position lines with those from terrestrial or electronic observations.

That is really all there is to the procedure for solving a sun sight, and most other celestial operations follow a similar pattern. The use of a standardized workform, as we have done for the sun, makes the process easy, and, as we explore the other navigational bodies, think in terms of the procedure you learned for the sun, and it will be easy to recognize the few exceptions.

7 The Moon

Since time immemorial, the moon has had an undeservedly poor reputation among navigators. I suspect that this is because of the moon's relative nearness to the earth, its changing size, and its irregular motion, all of which made sights of the moon much more laborious to reduce, and thus intensified the navigator's already burdensome existence. The natural response, perhaps, was simply to avoid the confrontation.

With today's almanac and modern inspection tables, there is no longer any justification for concern over moon sights; in fact, they can be particularly uesful at times. Quite often, one of the moon's limbs is sufficiently well defined during daylight hours to permit simultaneous observations of the moon and the sun for an immediate fix, and because of the moon's luminosity, sights at twilight may be possible while the horizon is still comparatively bright, producing results superior to those from any of the lesser bodies. During World War II, submarine navigators, using sextant eyepieces with exceptional light-gathering ability, were able to take moon sights when they surfaced at night, and occasionally, star sights over the moon-illuminated horizon. If you decide to try this yourself, let me caution that it is sometimes difficult to separate the true horizon from a false horizon that often appears under a low moon, so judge your results accordingly.

The best way to introduce yourself to moon observations is, as in the case of the sun, to work through a practical example. You will be glad to know that our procedure for working a moon sight is quite similar to that for the sun, using the same six basic steps, with only a few exceptions which I will point out as we proceed. Let's assume that you are the navigator, and some five hours after you took your sun line, your vessel has moved to a DR position at Latitude 41°08′N, Longitude 69°31′W, in the vicinity of Nantucket Shoals. At Greenwich mean time 20:57:09 on June 8, 1984, you make an observation of the moon's upper limb at a sextant altitude of 22°50.6′. A time-tick shows your watch to be 1 second slow; the index correction is still –2.4′, and the height of eye, 9 feet.

As in the case of your sun line, it is easiest to work with a standardized workform, and the one for the moon requires only minor changes from the one with which you are already familiar. On page 42, the moon sight in our practical example is shown in completed form; we will walk through the steps one at a time, so you can follow each one.

A sextant observation of the moon is made in exactly the same way as for the sun, bringing either the lower or upper limb (whichever is best defined and will produce the better sight) down to tangency with the horizon. The corrections for index error and dip also follow the sun procedure to obtain the apparent altitude, but then, to correct the apparent altitude, ha, to the observed altitude, Ho, you must use the moon tables inside the *back* cover of the *Nautical Almanac*, an example of which is seen in Figure 7–1.

DATE		June 8, 1984
BODY		Moon ☾
hs		22-50.6
IC		-2.4
D		-2.9
ha		22-45.3
R		+61.5
H.P.	H. P.	+4.6 (59.2)
(−30′)		-30.0
Ho		23-21.4
W		20-57-09
corr		+01
GMT		20-57-10
gha	v	0-34.2 (11.5)
incr		13-38.4
v corr		11.0
GHA		14-23.6
		+360
		374-23.6
aλ		-69-23.6
LHA		305
dec	d	2-46.5 S (15.4)
d corr		+14.8
Dec		3-01.3 S
a L		41 N
Tab Hc		23-27.0
corr		-01
Hc		23-26.0
Ho		23-21.4
a		4.6 A
Zn		117°

In the first part of the workform, the index correction of –2.4′, and the dip correction for a 9-foot height of eye—found in the dip table to be –2.9′—are applied to the sextant altitude, hs, to obtain the apparent altitude, ha, of 22°45.3′. To convert ha to Ho, you then enter the main body of the table, which presents the correction in two

App. Alt.	0°–4° Corr^n	5°–9° Corr^n	10°–14° Corr^n	15°–19° Corr^n	20°–24° Corr^n	25°–29° Corr^n	30°–34° Corr^n	App. Alt.
00	0° 33.8	5° 58.2	10° 62.1	15° 62.8	20° 62.2	25° 60.8	30° 58.9	00
10	35.9	58.5	62.2	62.8	62.1	60.8	58.8	10
20	37.8	58.7	62.2	62.8	62.1	60.7	58.8	20
30	39.6	58.9	62.3	62.8	62.1	60.7	58.7	30
40	41.2	59.1	62.3	62.8	62.0	60.6	58.6	40
50	42.6	59.3	62.4	62.7	62.0	60.6	58.5	50
00	1 44.0	6 59.5	11 62.4	16 62.7	21 62.0	26 60.5	31 58.5	00
10	45.2	59.7	62.4	62.7	61.9	60.4	58.4	10
20	46.3	59.9	62.5	62.7	61.9	60.4	58.3	20
30	47.3	60.0	62.5	62.7	61.9	60.3	58.2	30
40	48.3	60.2	62.5	62.7	61.8	60.3	58.2	40
50	49.2	60.3	62.6	62.7	61.8	60.2	58.1	50
00	2 50.0	7 60.5	12 62.6	17 62.7	22 61.7	27 60.1	32 58.0	00
10	50.8	60.6	62.6	62.6	61.7	60.1	57.9	10
20	51.4	60.7	62.6	62.6	61.6	60.0	57.8	20
30	52.1	60.9	62.7	62.6	61.6	59.9	57.8	30
40	52.7	61.0	62.7	62.6	61.5	59.9	57.7	40
50	53.3	61.1	62.7	62.6	61.5	59.8	57.6	50
00	3 53.8	8 61.2	13 62.7	18 62.5	23 61.5	28 59.7	33 57.5	00
10	54.3	61.3	62.7	62.5	61.4	59.7	57.4	10
20	54.8	61.4	62.7	62.5	61.4	59.6	57.4	20
30	55.2	61.5	62.8	62.5	61.3	59.6	57.3	30
40	55.6	61.6	62.8	62.4	61.3	59.5	57.2	40
50	56.0	61.6	62.8	62.4	61.2	59.4	57.1	50
00	4 56.4	9 61.7	14 62.8	19 62.4	24 61.2	29 59.3	34 57.0	00
10	56.7	61.8	62.8	62.3	61.1	59.3	56.9	10
20	57.1	61.9	62.8	62.3	61.1	59.2	56.9	20
30	57.4	61.9	62.8	62.3	61.0	59.1	56.8	30
40	57.7	62.0	62.8	62.2	60.9	59.1	56.7	40
50	57.9	62.1	62.8	62.2	60.9	59.0	56.6	50

H.P.	L	U	L	U	L	U	L	U	L	U	L	U	L	U	H.P.
54.0	0.3	0.9	0.3	0.9	0.4	1.0	0.5	1.1	0.6	1.2	0.7	1.3	0.9	1.5	54.0
54.3	0.7	1.1	0.7	1.2	0.7	1.2	0.8	1.3	0.9	1.4	1.1	1.5	1.2	1.7	54.3
54.6	1.1	1.4	1.1	1.4	1.1	1.4	1.2	1.5	1.3	1.6	1.4	1.7	1.5	1.8	54.6
54.9	1.4	1.6	1.5	1.6	1.5	1.6	1.6	1.7	1.6	1.8	1.8	1.9	1.9	2.0	54.9
55.2	1.8	1.8	1.8	1.8	1.9	1.9	1.9	1.9	2.0	2.0	2.1	2.1	2.2	2.2	55.2
55.5	2.2	2.0	2.2	2.0	2.3	2.1	2.3	2.1	2.4	2.2	2.4	2.3	2.5	2.4	55.5
55.8	2.6	2.2	2.6	2.2	2.6	2.3	2.7	2.3	2.7	2.4	2.8	2.4	2.9	2.5	55.8
56.1	3.0	2.4	3.0	2.5	3.0	2.5	3.0	2.5	3.1	2.6	3.1	2.6	3.2	2.7	56.1
56.4	3.4	2.7	3.4	2.7	3.4	2.7	3.4	2.7	3.4	2.8	3.5	2.8	3.5	2.9	56.4
56.7	3.7	2.9	3.7	2.9	3.8	2.9	3.8	2.9	3.8	3.0	3.8	3.0	3.9	3.0	56.7
57.0	4.1	3.1	4.1	3.1	4.1	3.1	4.1	3.1	4.2	3.1	4.2	3.2	4.2	3.2	57.0
57.3	4.5	3.3	4.5	3.3	4.5	3.3	4.5	3.3	4.5	3.3	4.5	3.4	4.6	3.4	57.3
57.6	4.9	3.5	4.9	3.5	4.9	3.5	4.9	3.5	4.9	3.5	4.9	3.5	4.9	3.6	57.6
57.9	5.3	3.8	5.3	3.8	5.2	3.8	5.2	3.7	5.2	3.7	5.2	3.7	5.2	3.7	57.9
58.2	5.6	4.0	5.6	4.0	5.6	4.0	5.6	4.0	5.6	3.9	5.6	3.9	5.6	3.9	58.2
58.5	6.0	4.2	6.0	4.2	6.0	4.2	6.0	4.2	6.0	4.1	5.9	4.1	5.9	4.1	58.5
58.8	6.4	4.4	6.4	4.4	6.4	4.4	6.3	4.4	6.3	4.3	6.3	4.3	6.2	4.2	58.8
59.1	6.8	4.6	6.8	4.6	6.7	4.6	6.7	4.6	6.7	4.5	6.6	4.5	6.6	4.4	59.1
59.4	7.2	4.8	7.1	4.8	7.1	4.8	7.1	4.8	7.0	4.7	7.0	4.7	6.9	4.6	59.4
59.7	7.5	5.1	7.5	5.0	7.5	5.0	7.5	5.0	7.4	4.9	7.3	4.8	7.2	4.7	59.7
60.0	7.9	5.3	7.9	5.3	7.9	5.2	7.8	5.2	7.8	5.1	7.7	5.0	7.6	4.9	60.0
60.3	8.3	5.5	8.3	5.5	8.2	5.4	8.2	5.4	8.1	5.3	8.0	5.2	7.9	5.1	60.3
60.6	8.7	5.7	8.7	5.7	8.6	5.7	8.6	5.6	8.5	5.5	8.4	5.4	8.2	5.3	60.6
60.9	9.1	5.9	9.0	5.9	9.0	5.9	8.9	5.8	8.8	5.7	8.7	5.6	8.6	5.4	60.9
61.2	9.5	6.2	9.4	6.1	9.4	6.1	9.3	6.0	9.2	5.9	9.1	5.8	8.9	5.6	61.2
61.5	9.8	6.4	9.8	6.3	9.7	6.3	9.7	6.2	9.5	6.1	9.4	5.9	9.2	5.8	61.5

DIP

Ht. of Eye	Corr^n	Ht. of Eye	Ht. of Eye	Corr^n	Ht. of Eye
m		ft.	m		ft.
2.4		8.0	9.5		31.5
	−2.8			−5.5	
2.6		8.6	9.9		32.7
	2.9			5.6	
2.8		9.2	10.3		33.9
	3.0			5.7	
3.0		9.8	10.6		35.1
	3.1			5.8	
3.2		10.5	11.0		36.3
	3.2			5.9	
3.4		11.2	11.4		37.6
	3.3			6.0	
3.6		11.9	11.8		38.9
	3.4			6.1	
3.8		12.6	12.2		40.1
	3.5			6.2	
4.0		13.3	12.6		41.5
	3.6			6.3	
4.3		14.1	13.0		42.8
	3.7			6.4	
4.5		14.9	13.4		44.2
	3.8			6.5	
4.7		15.7	13.8		45.5
	3.9			6.6	
5.0		16.5	14.2		46.9
	4.0			6.7	
5.2		17.4	14.7		48.4
	4.1			6.8	
5.5		18.3	15.1		49.8
	4.2			6.9	
5.8		19.1	15.5		51.3
	4.3			7.0	
6.1		20.1	16.0		52.8
	4.4			7.1	
6.3		21.0	16.5		54.3
	4.5			7.2	
6.6		22.0	16.9		55.8
	4.6			7.3	
6.9		22.9	17.4		57.4
	4.7			7.4	
7.2		23.9	17.9		58.9
	4.8			7.5	
7.5		24.9	18.4		60.5
	4.9			7.6	
7.9		26.0	18.8		62.1
	5.0			7.7	
8.2		27.1	19.3		63.8
	5.1			7.8	
8.5		28.1	19.8		65.4
	5.2			7.9	
8.8		29.2	20.4		67.1
	5.3			8.0	
9.2		30.4	20.9		68.8
	5.4			8.1	
9.5		31.5	21.4		70.5

MOON CORRECTION TABLE

The correction is in two parts; the first correction is taken from the upper part of the table with argument apparent altitude, and the second from the lower part, with argument H.P., in the same column as that from which the first correction was taken. Separate corrections are given in the lower part for lower (L) and upper (U) limbs. All corrections are to be **added** to apparent altitude, *but 30′ is to be subtracted from the altitude of the upper limb.*

For corrections for pressure and temperature see page A4.

For bubble sextant observations ignore dip, take the mean of upper and lower limb corrections and subtract 15′ from the altitude.

App. Alt. = Apparent altitude = Sextant altitude corrected for index error and dip.

Figure 7–1. **Moon altitude correction tables from the *Nautical Almanac.* Note that all corrections are additive, but that 30′ must be subtracted from observations of the moon's upper limb.**

parts. The first, or R-correction, is taken from the upper half of the table by descending the column in which the degrees of apparent altitude appear, to the reading opposite the minutes of ha. Interpolation, if any is necessary, can be done by eye. In our example, descending the column headed 20°–24°, under 22° and opposite 40′ you will see the value 61.5′. Since this value remains the same for all minutes between 40′ and 50′, no interpolation is needed, and so, for our apparent altitude of 22°45.3′, the R-correction is 61.5′.

The second, or H.P.-correction, is for horizontal parallax. Horizontal parallax is the difference in altitude between that measured from the observer's position on the earth's surface, and that measured from the center of the earth. A correction for H.P. is necessary only for moon sights; all the other celestial bodies are far enough away to make the correction negligible. The amount of the H.P.-correction is found by descending the same column as for the first, R-correction, into the lower half of the table—under the heading L, for lower limb, or U, for upper limb—to the reading opposite the value for H.P., which you will find in the daily pages of the almanac as will be described momentarily. In our moon sight, we had chosen to use the upper limb for our observation, and the horizontal parallax had been found in the almanac to be 59.2′. Descending the 20°–24° column in Figure 7–1, under the U-heading, you can see that the value for an H.P.of 59.1′ would be 4.5′, and for an H.P. of 59.4′, it would be 4.7′. Interpolating by eye, you arrive at an H.P.-correction of 4.6′ for our H.P. of 59.2′ as entered on the workform.

Both of the moon-table corrections are added to the apparent altitude, but in the case of observations of the moon's upper limb, 30′ must be subtracted from the total. Accordingly, when our R-, H.P.-, and upper-limb corrections are all applied to the apparent altitude of 22°45.3′, the resulting observed altitude, Ho, becomes 23°21.4′.

As in the procedure for our sun sight, the observed altitude is set aside while we turn to the almanac for the needed astronomical data. It is here, when you open to the appropriate daily page to find the moon's Greenwich hour angle and declination (Figure 7–2), that you will find, in the moon's fifth column opposite the nearest hour of Greenwich mean time, the H.P. (59.2′). This is the value that is used for the second half of the altitude correction, and you will notice that I have included a small box in which to record it on my suggested workform.

1984 JUNE 8, 9, 10 (FRI., SAT., SUN.)

G.M.T.		SUN		MOON				
		G.H.A.	Dec.	G.H.A.	v	Dec.	d	H.P.
d	h	° ′	° ′	° ′	′	° ′	′	′
8	00	180 15.9	N22 50.6	70 23.2	11.5	N 2 23.8	15.5	59.3
	01	195 15.8	50.9	84 53.7	11.5	2 08.3	15.5	59.3
	02	210 15.7	51.1	99 24.2	11.5	1 52.8	15.5	59.3
	03	225 15.5	· · 51.3	113 54.7	11.6	1 37.3	15.6	59.3
	04	240 15.4	51.5	128 25.3	11.5	1 21.7	15.5	59.3
	05	255 15.3	51.8	142 55.8	11.5	1 06.2	15.5	59.3
	06	270 15.2	N22 52.0	157 26.3	11.6	N 0 50.7	15.5	59.3
	07	285 15.1	52.2	171 56.9	11.6	0 35.2	15.6	59.3
	08	300 14.9	52.4	186 27.5	11.5	0 19.6	15.5	59.3
F	09	315 14.8	· · 52.6	200 58.0	11.6	N 0 04.1	15.6	59.3
R	10	330 14.7	52.9	215 28.6	11.6	S 0 11.5	15.5	59.3
I	11	345 14.6	53.1	229 59.2	11.5	0 27.0	15.5	59.3
D	12	0 14.5	N22 53.3	244 29.7	11.6	S 0 42.5	15.5	59.3
A	13	15 14.3	53.5	259 00.3	11.6	0 58.0	15.6	59.3
Y	14	30 14.2	53.7	273 30.9	11.5	1 13.6	15.5	59.3
	15	45 14.1	· · 54.0	288 01.4	11.6	1 29.1	15.5	59.3
	16	60 14.0	54.2	302 32.0	11.5	1 44.6	15.5	59.3
	17	75 13.9	54.4	317 02.5	11.6	2 00.1	15.4	59.3
	18	90 13.7	N22 54.6	331 33.1	11.5	S 2 15.5	15.5	59.3
	19	105 13.6	54.8	346 03.6	11.6	2 31.0	15.5	59.3
	20	120 13.5	55.0	0 34.2	11.5	2 46.5	15.4	59.2
	21	135 13.4	· · 55.2	15 04.7	11.5	3 01.9	15.4	59.2
	22	150 13.3	55.4	29 35.2	11.5	3 17.3	15.4	59.2
	23	165 13.1	55.7	44 05.7	11.5	3 32.7	15.4	59.2

Figure 7–2. **Excerpt from the *Nautical Almanac* showing astronomical data for the moon on June 8, 1984, at 20h GMT**

A moon sight is timed in exactly the same way as in an observation of the sun or any other celestial body, at the instant the reflected image of the body appears to touch the horizon. In our June 8 practical example, the watch again was set to Greenwich mean time, and it read 20:57:09 at the moment of the observation. In this case, however, we will assume that we had found, by an earlier radio time-tick, that our watch was reading 1 second slow, and so, as it shows in the workform, 1 second was added to correct the GMT of the observation to 20:57:10.

The almanac's daily page, an excerpt of which is shown in Figure 7–2, is entered in the same way as you did for the sun, except, of course, you use the MOON columns. In our example, the tabular Greenwich hour angle of 0°34.2′ is found opposite the hours of GMT; here, 20^h. Similarly, the increment for the 57 minutes and 10 seconds of time is found in the yellow *Increments and Corrections* table in the back of the almanac (Figure 7–3); be careful again to use the MOON column. In the case of the moon, there is a small, additional increment called the *v*-correction, which takes into account the excesses in the moon's irregular movement over the constant rate used in the increment table. The value of *v* is found in the second column of moon data (Figure 7–2); at 20 hours Greenwich mean time on June 8, it is 11.5′, and a box has been provided on the workform to record it. Returning to the body of the workform, the first GHA increment of 13° 38.4′ (for 57^m10^s), and the small *v*-increment, found in the columns at the right of Figure 7–3 to be 11.0′ for a *v*-value of 11.5′, are added to the tabular Greenwich hour angle to obtain the final GHA for our observation: 14°23.6′.

The declination of the moon is found opposite the hour of observation in the third of the moon's daily-page columns, as seen in Figure 7–2. At 20 hours GMT, it is 2° 46.5′S. While this declination figure can be adjusted for minutes and seconds of time by inspection, as you did for the sun, it is usually quicker and easier to note the value

INCREMENTS AND CORRECTIONS 57m

57	SUN PLANETS	ARIES	MOON	v or d	Corrn	v or d	Corrn	v or d	Corrn
s	° ′	° ′	° ′	′	′	′	′	′	′
00	14 15·0	14 17·3	13 36·1	0·0	0·0	6·0	5·8	12·0	11·5
01	14 15·3	14 17·6	13 36·3	0·1	0·1	6·1	5·8	12·1	11·6
02	14 15·5	14 17·8	13 36·5	0·2	0·2	6·2	5·9	12·2	11·7
03	14 15·8	14 18·1	13 36·8	0·3	0·3	6·3	6·0	12·3	11·8
04	14 16·0	14 18·3	13 37·0	0·4	0·4	6·4	6·1	12·4	11·9
05	14 16·3	14 18·6	13 37·2	0·5	0·5	6·5	6·2	12·5	12·0
06	14 16·5	14 18·8	13 37·5	0·6	0·6	6·6	6·3	12·6	12·1
07	14 16·8	14 19·1	13 37·7	0·7	0·7	6·7	6·4	12·7	12·2
08	14 17·0	14 19·3	13 38·0	0·8	0·8	6·8	6·5	12·8	12·3
09	14 17·3	14 19·6	13 38·2	0·9	0·9	6·9	6·6	12·9	12·4
10	14 17·5	14 19·8	13 38·4	1·0	1·0	7·0	6·7	13·0	12·5
11	14 17·8	14 20·1	13 38·7	1·1	1·1	7·1	6·8	13·1	12·6
12	14 18·0	14 20·3	13 38·9	1·2	1·2	7·2	6·9	13·2	12·7
13	14 18·3	14 20·6	13 39·2	1·3	1·2	7·3	7·0	13·3	12·7
14	14 18·5	14 20·9	13 39·4	1·4	1·3	7·4	7·1	13·4	12·8
15	14 18·8	14 21·1	13 39·6	1·5	1·4	7·5	7·2	13·5	12·9
16	14 19·0	14 21·4	13 39·9	1·6	1·5	7·6	7·3	13·6	13·0
17	14 19·3	14 21·6	13 40·1	1·7	1·6	7·7	7·4	13·7	13·1
18	14 19·5	14 21·9	13 40·3	1·8	1·7	7·8	7·5	13·8	13·2
19	14 19·8	14 22·1	13 40·6	1·9	1·8	7·9	7·6	13·9	13·3
20	14 20·0	14 22·4	13 40·8	2·0	1·9	8·0	7·7	14·0	13·4
21	14 20·3	14 22·6	13 41·1	2·1	2·0	8·1	7·8	14·1	13·5
22	14 20·5	14 22·9	13 41·3	2·2	2·1	8·2	7·9	14·2	13·6
23	14 20·8	14 23·1	13 41·5	2·3	2·2	8·3	8·0	14·3	13·7
24	14 21·0	14 23·4	13 41·8	2·4	2·3	8·4	8·1	14·4	13·8
25	14 21·3	14 23·6	13 42·0	2·5	2·4	8·5	8·1	14·5	13·9
26	14 21·5	14 23·9	13 42·3	2·6	2·5	8·6	8·2	14·6	14·0
27	14 21·8	14 24·1	13 42·5	2·7	2·6	8·7	8·3	14·7	14·1
28	14 22·0	14 24·4	13 42·7	2·8	2·7	8·8	8·4	14·8	14·2
29	14 22·3	14 24·6	13 43·0	2·9	2·8	8·9	8·5	14·9	14·3
30	14 22·5	14 24·9	13 43·2	3·0	2·9	9·0	8·6	15·0	14·4
31	14 22·8	14 25·1	13 43·4	3·1	3·0	9·1	8·7	15·1	14·5
32	14 23·0	14 25·4	13 43·7	3·2	3·1	9·2	8·8	15·2	14·6
33	14 23·3	14 25·6	13 43·9	3·3	3·2	9·3	8·9	15·3	14·7
34	14 23·5	14 25·9	13 44·2	3·4	3·3	9·4	9·0	15·4	14·8
35	14 23·8	14 26·1	13 44·4	3·5	3·4	9·5	9·1	15·5	14·9
36	14 24·0	14 26·4	13 44·6	3·6	3·5	9·6	9·2	15·6	15·0
37	14 24·3	14 26·6	13 44·9	3·7	3·5	9·7	9·3	15·7	15·0
38	14 24·5	14 26·9	13 45·1	3·8	3·6	9·8	9·4	15·8	15·1
39	14 24·8	14 27·1	13 45·4	3·9	3·7	9·9	9·5	15·9	15·2
40	14 25·0	14 27·4	13 45·6	4·0	3·8	10·0	9·6	16·0	15·3
41	14 25·3	14 27·6	13 45·8	4·1	3·9	10·1	9·7	16·1	15·4
42	14 25·5	14 27·9	13 46·1	4·2	4·0	10·2	9·8	16·2	15·5
43	14 25·8	14 28·1	13 46·3	4·3	4·1	10·3	9·9	16·3	15·6
44	14 26·0	14 28·4	13 46·5	4·4	4·2	10·4	10·0	16·4	15·7
45	14 26·3	14 28·6	13 46·8	4·5	4·3	10·5	10·1	16·5	15·8
46	14 26·5	14 28·9	13 47·0	4·6	4·4	10·6	10·2	16·6	15·9
47	14 26·8	14 29·1	13 47·3	4·7	4·5	10·7	10·3	16·7	16·0
48	14 27·0	14 29·4	13 47·5	4·8	4·6	10·8	10·4	16·8	16·1
49	14 27·3	14 29·6	13 47·7	4·9	4·7	10·9	10·4	16·9	16·2
50	14 27·5	14 29·9	13 48·0	5·0	4·8	11·0	10·5	17·0	16·3
51	14 27·8	14 30·1	13 48·2	5·1	4·9	11·1	10·6	17·1	16·4
52	14 28·0	14 30·4	13 48·5	5·2	5·0	11·2	10·7	17·2	16·5
53	14 28·3	14 30·6	13 48·7	5·3	5·1	11·3	10·8	17·3	16·6
54	14 28·5	14 30·9	13 48·9	5·4	5·2	11·4	10·9	17·4	16·7
55	14 28·8	14 31·1	13 49·2	5·5	5·3	11·5	11·0	17·5	16·8
56	14 29·0	14 31·4	13 49·4	5·6	5·4	11·6	11·1	17·6	16·9
57	14 29·3	14 31·6	13 49·7	5·7	5·5	11·7	11·2	17·7	17·0
58	14 29·5	14 31·9	13 49·9	5·8	5·6	11·8	11·3	17·8	17·1
59	14 29·8	14 32·1	13 50·1	5·9	5·7	11·9	11·4	17·9	17·2
60	14 30·0	14 32·4	13 50·4	6·0	5·8	12·0	11·5	18·0	17·3

Figure 7–3. **Excerpt from the *Nautical Almanac's Increments and Corrections* tables indicating the GHA increment for 57m10s, and the appropriate *v* and *d* corrections**

for *d* (which represents the hourly change in declination) in the fourth column of the moon data, and enter that value in the increment table in the same way as you did for the *v*-increment. In our example, the *d*-correction at 57 minutes for a *d*-value of 15.4′ is 14.8′. When this correction is applied to the tabular declination, the final declination for $20^h57^m10^s$ GMT becomes 3°01.3′S. Unlike the *v*-increment, which is always additive, it is necessary to check whether the declination is increasing or decreasing (in our example, it is the former), so that you apply the *d*-correction with the proper sign.

With the extra altitude adjustment, the additional hour-angle correction, and, if you wish, using the *d*-correction to adjust the declination, the special treatment of a moon sight is now complete. For clarity, I have described each step in detail, but you will soon find that with a workform and a little practice the few extra requirements of a moon sight quickly become routine. The remaining steps in deriving the moon's line of position are identical with the procedure you followed with the sun.

Having obtained the Greenwich hour angle, you must next apply your assumed longitude (selecting it to come out to a whole degree) to arrive at the local hour angle. The DR position in our example is 69°31′W, so 69°23.6′W would be appropriate for an assumed longitude, but, as in the case of our sun sight, *a*λ is larger than GHA, so 360° must be added to the GHA before the subtraction (required, you will remember, because the longitude is West) can take place. The workform shows the calculations resulting in a local hour angle of 305°. We now have the LHA (305°), the declination (3°01.3′S), and assume a latitude (41°) near our DR latitude of 41°08′N, the three values needed to enter the sight reduction table. An excerpt of the applicable page from Pub. No. 249, Volume III, is shown in Figure 7–4. Note that since the declina-

A greater than 180°........Zn=Z
A less than 180°...........Zn=360−Z DECLINATION (0°-14°) CONTRARY NAME TO LATITUDE

LAT 41°

°	1°			2°			3°			4°			5°				13°			14°			
Z	Hc	d	Z	Hc	d	Z	Hc	d	Z	Hc	d	Z	Hc	d	d	Z	Hc	d	Z	Hc	d	Z	LHA
104	15 01	42	105	14 19	41	106	13 38	41	106	12 57	42	107	12 15	41	42	113	06 40	43	114	05 57	42	114	291
105	15 44	41	106	15 03	41	106	14 22	42	107	13 40	42	108	12 58	4	42	114	07 21	43	114	06 38	42	115	292
106	16 28	42	106	15 46	41	107	15 05	42	108	14 23	42	109	13 41	4	43	114	08 02	43	115	07 19	43	116	293
106	17 11	41	107	16 30	42	108	15 48	42	109	15 06	42	109	14 24	[illegible]	43	115	08 43	43	116	08 00	43	117	294
107	17 54	−41	108	17 13	−42	109	16 31	−42	109	15 49	−43	110	15 06	−	−43	116	09 24	−44	117	08 40	−43	117	295
108	18 37	42	109	17 55	42	109	17 13	42	110	16 31	43	111	15 48	4	43	117	10 04	44	117	09 20	43	118	296
109	19 20	42	109	18 38	42	110	17 56	43	111	17 13	42	112	16 31	4	44	117	10 44	44	118	10 00	44	119	297
109	20 03	42	110	19 21	43	111	18 38	43	112	17 55	43	112	17 12	43	44	118	11 24	44	119	10 40	44	119	298
110	20 45	42	111	20 03	43	112	19 20	43	112	18 37	43	113	17 54	43	4	119	12 04	45	119	11 19	44	120	299
111	21 28	−43	112	20 45	−43	112	20 02	−43	113	19 19	−44	114	18 35	−43	4	119	12 43	−45	120	11 58	−44	121	300
112	22 10	43	112	21 27	44	113	20 43	43	114	20 00	44	115	19 16	43		120	13 22	45	121	12 37	45	122	301
112	22 51	43	113	22 08	43	114	21 25	44	115	20 41	44	115	19 57	44		121	14 01	45	122	13 16	46	122	302
113	23 33	44	114	22 49	43	115	22 06	44	115	21 22	44	116	20 38	45		122	14 39	45	122	13 54	46	123	303
114	24 14	43	115	23 31	44	115	22 47	45	116	22 02	44	117	21 18	45		123	15 17	46	123	14 31	45	124	304
115	24 55	−44	115	24 11	−44	116	23 27	−44	117	22 43	−45	118	21 58	−45	6	123	15 55	−46	124	15 09	−46	125	305
116	25 36	44	116	24 52	45	117	24 07	44	118	23 23	45	119	22 38	45	17	124	16 32	46	125	15 46	46	125	306
116	26 17	45	117	25 32	45	118	24 47	45	119	24 02	45	119	23 17	45	47	125	17 09	46	126	16 23	47	126	307
117	26 57	45	118	26 12	45	119	25 27	45	119	24 42	46	120	23 56	46	47	126	17 46	47	126	16 59	47	127	308
118	27 37	46	119	26 51	45	120	26 06	45	120	25 21	46	121	24 35	46	48	126	18 22	47	127	17 35	47	128	309

Figure 7–4. **Excerpt from Pub. No. 249, Volume III, showing the values for Latitude 41°N, Declination 3°S, and LHA 305 to be: Hc 23°27′, *d* −44′, Z 117°**

tion is South, while the assumed latitude is North, the table headed "Declination Contrary Name to Latitude" has been selected.

In the same manner as for the sun, enter the column for 3° declination, and, opposite the LHA of 305°, extract the three values: Hc 23°27′, *d* −44′, and Z 117°. The tabular value for Hc needs to be adjusted for the incremental minutes of declination (here, 01.3′), and this is done in Table 5, excerpted in Figure 7–5. In our practical example, the altitude differential, *d*, of −44′, applied to 1′ of declination, yields a correction of −01′ to the tabular altitude, making the final Hc 23°26.0′. This Hc is then compared with the observed altitude, Ho, which we

TABLE 5.—Correction to Tabulated Altitude

41	42	43	44	45	46	47	48	49	50	51	52	53	54	55	56	57	58	59	60	d / ′
0	0	0	0	0	0	0	0	0	0	0	0	0	0	0	0	0	0	0	0	0
1	1	1	1	1	1	1	1	1	1	1	1	1	1	1	1	1	1	1	1	1
1	1	1	1	2	2	2	2	2	2	2	2	2	2	2	2	2	2	2	2	2
2	2	2	2	2	2	2	2	2	2	3	3	3	3	3	3	3	3	3	3	3
3	3	3	3	3	3	3	3	3	3	3	3	4	4	4	4	4	4	4	4	4
3	4	4	4	4	4	4	4	4	4	4	4	4	4	5	5	5	5	5	5	5
4	4	4	4	4	5	5	5	5	5	5	5	5	5	6	6	6	6	6	6	6
5	5	5	5	5	5	5	6	6	6	6	6	6	6	6	7	7	7	7	7	7
5	6	6	6	6	6	6	6	7	7	7	7	7	7	7	7	8	8	8	8	8
6	6	6	7	7	7	7	7	7	8	8	8	8	8	8	8	9	9	9	9	9
7	7	7	7	8	8	8	8	8	8	8	9	9	9	9	9	10	10	10	10	10
8	8	8	8	8	8	9	9	9	9	9	10	10	10	10	10	10	11	11	11	11
8	8	9	9	9	9	9	10	10	10	10	10	11	11	11	11	11	12	12	12	12
9	9	9	10	10	10	10	10	11	11	11	11	11	12	12	12	12	13	13	13	13
10	10	10	10	10	11	11	11	11	12	12	12	12	13	13	13	13	14	14	14	14

***Figure 7–5.* Excerpt from Table 5, Pub. No. 249, showing a correction of 01′ for *d* of 44, and incremental minutes of declination, 01**

determined earlier, to arrive at the intercept, a. Since Hc in our example is greater than Ho, the intercept of 4.6′ is "away." Applying the rule in the upper corner of the sight reduction table (Figure 7–4), with an LHA of 305° the true azimuth, Zn, is equal to the azimuth angle, Z, so our azimuth line for plotting is 117°.

The final step is to plot the intercept from the assumed position; in our example in the direction opposite the azimuth ("away"). At the end of the intercept, the line of position is constructed at right angles to the azimuth line. Label the position line, and your moon sight is recorded for posterity.

Many present-day navigators find moon sights to be second only to sun lines, so forget the problems of the ancients, and try the moon yourself. The reward is well worth the few extra steps this valuable body requires.

8 The Planets

Four major planets are of interest to celestial navigators: Venus, Mars, Jupiter, and Saturn. As for the sun and moon, the *Nautical Almanac*'s daily pages present the complete astronomical data for each of these planets for each whole hour of Greenwich mean time. Planet information is found on the left-hand page, or "star side" of the almanac, an example of which is shown in Figure 8–1.

Of the four planets, Venus is the most distinctive. Not only is it the brightest body in the heavens besides the sun and moon, but it is also easy to identify as a morning or evening "star," never far from the sun. Under ideal conditions, Venus can be seen in the daytime, offering an opportunity for a simultaneous fix by the observation of two celestial bodies. Jupiter is also quite brilliant, often being brighter than Sirius, the brightest of the stars, but while it can occasionally be observed in daylight, Jupiter frequently provides excellent sights at morning or evening twilight. Mars and Saturn are more difficult to distinguish from the stars at twilight, and you may find it best to work through a quick trial reduction, obtaining an approximate altitude and azimuth to help find them.

As we did with the sun and moon, let's work through

1984 OCTOBER 18, 19, 20 (THURS., FRI., SAT.)

G.M.T.		ARIES	VENUS −3.4		MARS +0.6		JUPITER −1.7		SATURN +0.8		STARS		
d	h	G.H.A.	G.H.A.	Dec.	G.H.A.	Dec.	G.H.A.	Dec.	G.H.A.	Dec.	Name	S.H.A.	Dec.
18	00	26 39.8	151 53.2	S20 24.2	106 47.4	S25 08.9	109 21.6	S23 25.4	162 18.7	S14 42.6	Acamar	315 34.5	S40 21
	01	41 42.3	166 52.6	25.0	121 47.9	08.7	124 23.6	25.4	177 20.9	42.7	Achernar	335 42.2	S57 18
	02	56 44.8	181 51.9	25.8	136 48.4	08.6	139 25.7	25.4	192 23.1	42.8	Acrux	173 34.8	S63 00
	03	71 47.2	196 51.2	26.6	151 48.9	08.4	154 27.8	25.3	207 25.3	42.8	Adhara	255 29.7	S28 56
	04	86 49.7	211 50.6	27.4	166 49.4	08.3	169 29.9	25.3	222 27.4	42.9	Aldebaran	291 14.3	N16 28
	05	101 52.2	226 49.9	28.2	181 49.9	08.1	184 32.0	25.3	237 29.6	43.0			
	06	116 54.6	241 49.2	S20 29.0	196 50.4	S25 08.0	199 34.1	S23 25.3	252 31.8	S14 43.1	Alioth	166 40.2	N56 02
	07	131 57.1	256 48.6	29.9	211 50.9	07.8	214 36.2	25.3	267 34.0	43.2	Alkaid	153 16.5	N49 23
T	08	146 59.5	271 47.9	30.7	226 51.4	07.7	229 38.3	25.3	282 36.2	43.3	Al Na'ir	28 10.8	S47 02
H	09	162 02.0	286 47.2	31.5	241 51.9	07.5	244 40.3	25.3	297 38.3	43.3	Alnilam	276 08.4	S 1 12
U	10	177 04.5	301 46.5	32.3	256 52.4	07.4	259 42.4	25.2	312 40.5	43.4	Alphard	218 17.8	S 8 35
R	11	192 06.9	316 45.9	33.1	271 52.9	07.2	274 44.5	25.2	327 42.7	43.5			
S	12	207 09.4	331 45.2	S20 33.9	286 53.4	S25 07.1	289 46.6	S23 25.2	342 44.9	S14 43.6	Alphecca	126 29.9	N26 46
D	13	222 11.9	346 44.5	34.7	301 53.9	06.9	304 48.7	25.2	357 47.1	43.7	Alpheratz	358 06.0	N29 00
A	14	237 14.3	1 43.8	35.5	316 54.4	06.8	319 50.8	25.2	12 49.3	43.8	Altair	62 29.6	N 8 49
Y	15	252 16.8	16 43.2	36.3	331 54.9	06.6	334 52.9	25.2	27 51.4	43.9	Ankaa	353 36.7	S42 23
	16	267 19.3	31 42.5	37.1	346 55.4	06.5	349 55.0	25.2	42 53.6	43.9	Antares	112 53.5	S26 24
	17	282 21.7	46 41.8	37.9	1 55.9	06.3	4 57.0	25.1	57 55.8	44.0			
	18	297 24.2	61 41.1	S20 38.7	16 56.4	S25 06.1	19 59.1	S23 25.1	72 58.0	S14 44.1	Arcturus	146 16.0	N19 15
	19	312 26.6	76 40.5	39.5	31 56.9	06.0	35 01.2	25.1	88 00.2	44.2	Atria	108 15.5	S69 00
	20	327 29.1	91 39.8	40.3	46 57.4	05.8	50 03.3	25.1	103 02.3	44.3	Avior	234 27.2	S59 27
	21	342 31.6	106 39.1	41.1	61 57.9	05.7	65 05.4	25.1	118 04.5	44.4	Bellatrix	278 55.3	N 6 20
	22	357 34.0	121 38.4	41.9	76 58.4	05.5	80 07.5	25.1	133 06.7	44.5	Betelgeuse	271 24.9	N 7 24
	23	12 36.5	136 37.7	42.7	91 58.9	05.4	95 09.5	25.1	148 08.9	44.5			
19	00	27 39.0	151 37.1	S20 43.5	106 59.4	S25 05.2	110 11.6	S23 25.0	163 11.1	S14 44.6	Canopus	264 05.7	S52 40
	01	42 41.4	166 36.4	44.3	121 59.9	05.0	125 13.7	25.0	178 13.3	44.7	Capella	281 06.6	N45 59
	02	57 43.9	181 35.7	45.1	137 00.4	04.9	140 15.8	25.0	193 15.4	44.8	Deneb	49 46.4	N45 13
	03	72 46.4	196 35.0	45.9	152 00.9	04.7	155 17.9	25.0	208 17.6	44.9	Denebola	182 56.2	N14 39
	04	87 48.8	211 34.3	46.7	167 01.5	04.6	170 20.0	25.0	223 19.8	45.0	Diphda	349 17.5	S18 04
	05	102 51.3	226 33.7	47.5	182 02.0	04.4	185 22.0	25.0	238 22.0	45.1			
	06	117 53.8	241 33.0	S20 48.3	197 02.5	S25 04.2	200 24.1	S23 25.0	253 24.2	S14 45.1	Dubhe	194 18.7	N61 50
	07	132 56.2	256 32.3	49.1	212 03.0	04.1	215 26.2	24.9	268 26.3	45.2	Elnath	278 40.1	N28 35
	08	147 58.7	271 31.6	49.8	227 03.5	03.9	230 28.3	24.9	283 28.5	45.3	Eltanin	90 56.6	N51 29
F	09	163 01.1	286 30.9	50.6	242 04.0	03.8	245 30.4	24.9	298 30.7	45.4	Enif	34 08.5	N 9 48
R	10	178 03.6	301 30.2	51.4	257 04.5	03.6	260 32.4	24.9	313 32.9	45.5	Fomalhaut	15 47.8	S29 42
I	11	193 06.1	316 29.6	52.2	272 05.0	03.4	275 34.5	24.9	328 35.1	45.6			
D	12	208 08.5	331 28.9	S20 53.0	287 05.5	S25 03.3	290 36.6	S23 24.9	343 37.2	S14 45.6	Gacrux	172 26.2	S57 01
A	13	223 11.0	346 28.2	53.8	302 06.0	03.1	305 38.7	24.8	358 39.4	45.7	Gienah	176 15.2	S17 27
Y	14	238 13.5	1 27.5	54.6	317 06.5	02.9	320 40.8	24.8	13 41.6	45.8	Hadar	149 20.0	S60 17
	15	253 15.9	16 26.8	55.3	332 07.0	02.8	335 42.8	24.8	28 43.8	45.9	Hamal	328 25.3	N23 23
	16	268 18.4	31 26.1	56.1	347 07.5	02.6	350 44.9	24.8	43 46.0	46.0	Kaus Aust.	84 13.0	S34 23
	17	283 20.9	46 25.4	56.9	2 08.0	02.4	5 47.0	24.8	58 48.1	46.1			
	18	298 23.3	61 24.7	S20 57.7	17 08.5	S25 02.3	20 49.1	S23 24.8	73 50.3	S14 46.2	Kochab	137 19.8	N74 13
	19	313 25.8	76 24.1	58.5	32 09.0	02.1	35 51.2	24.8	88 52.5	46.2	Markab	14 00.0	N15 07
	20	328 28.3	91 23.4	20 59.2	47 09.5	01.9	50 53.2	24.7	103 54.7	46.3	Menkar	314 37.7	N 4 01
	21	343 30.7	106 22.7	21 00.0	62 10.0	01.8	65 55.3	24.7	118 56.9	46.4	Menkent	148 34.0	S36 17
	22	358 33.2	121 22.0	00.8	77 10.5	01.6	80 57.4	24.7	133 59.0	46.5	Miaplacidus	221 44.9	S69 38
	23	13 35.6	136 21.3	01.6	92 11.0	01.4	95 59.5	24.7	149 01.2	46.6			
20	00	28 38.1	151 20.6	S21 02.3	107 11.5	S25 01.3	111 01.5	S23 24.7	164 03.4	S14 46.7	Mirfak	309 11.5	N49 48
	01	43 40.6	166 19.9	03.1	122 12.0	01.1	126 03.6	24.7	179 05.6	46.8	Nunki	76 25.5	S26 19
	02	58 43.0	181 19.2	03.9	137 12.5	00.9	141 05.7	24.7	194 07.8	46.8	Peacock	53 53.4	S56 47
	03	73 45.5	196 18.5	04.6	152 13.0	00.8	156 07.8	24.6	209 09.9	46.9	Pollux	243 54.5	N28 03
	04	88 48.0	211 17.8	05.4	167 13.5	00.6	171 09.9	24.6	224 12.1	47.0	Procyon	245 22.6	N 5 16
	05	103 50.4	226 17.1	06.2	182 14.0	00.4	186 11.9	24.6	239 14.3	47.1			
	06	118 52.9	241 16.4	S21 06.9	197 14.4	S25 00.3	201 14.0	S23 24.6	254 16.5	S14 47.2	Rasalhague	96 27.0	N12 34
	07	133 55.4	256 15.7	07.7	212 14.9	25 00.1	216 16.1	24.6	269 18.7	47.3	Regulus	208 07.0	N12 02
S	08	148 57.8	271 15.1	08.5	227 15.4	24 59.9	231 18.2	24.6	284 20.8	47.4	Rigel	281 32.9	S 8 12
A	09	164 00.3	286 14.4	09.2	242 15.9	59.7	246 20.2	24.5	299 23.0	47.4	Rigil Kent.	140 22.6	S60 46
T	10	179 02.8	301 13.7	10.0	257 16.4	59.6	261 22.3	24.5	314 25.2	47.5	Sabik	102 37.9	S15 42
U	11	194 05.2	316 13.0	10.8	272 16.9	59.4	276 24.4	24.5	329 27.4	47.6			
R	12	209 07.7	331 12.3	S21 11.5	287 17.4	S24 59.2	291 26.5	S23 24.5	344 29.6	S14 47.7	Schedar	350 05.3	N56 27
D	13	224 10.1	346 11.6	12.3	302 17.9	59.0	306 28.5	24.5	359 31.7	47.8	Shaula	96 51.9	S37 05
A	14	239 12.6	1 10.9	13.0	317 18.4	58.9	321 30.6	24.5	14 33.9	47.9	Sirius	258 53.0	S16 41
Y	15	254 15.1	16 10.2	13.8	332 18.9	58.7	336 32.7	24.5	29 36.1	48.0	Spica	158 54.7	S11 04
	16	269 17.5	31 09.5	14.6	347 19.4	58.5	351 34.7	24.4	44 38.3	48.0	Suhail	223 08.8	S43 21
	17	284 20.0	46 08.8	15.3	2 19.9	58.3	6 36.8	24.4	59 40.5	48.1			
	18	299 22.5	61 08.1	S21 16.1	17 20.4	S24 58.2	21 38.9	S23 24.4	74 42.6	S14 48.2	Vega	80 54.0	N38 46
	19	314 24.9	76 07.4	16.8	32 20.9	58.0	36 41.0	24.4	89 44.8	48.3	Zuben'ubi	137 30.1	S15 58
	20	329 27.4	91 06.7	17.6	47 21.4	57.8	51 43.0	24.4	104 47.0	48.4		S.H.A.	Mer. Pass.
	21	344 29.9	106 06.0	18.3	62 21.9	57.6	66 45.1	24.4	119 49.2	48.5		° ′	h m
	22	359 32.3	121 05.3	19.1	77 22.4	57.5	81 47.2	24.3	134 51.4	48.5	Venus	123 58.1	13 54
	23	14 34.8	136 04.6	19.8	92 22.9	57.3	96 49.3	24.3	149 53.5	48.6	Mars	79 20.5	16 51
Mer. Pass.		22 05.8	v −0.7	d 0.8	v 0.5	d 0.2	v 2.1	d 0.0	v 2.2	d 0.1	Jupiter	82 32.7	16 37
											Saturn	135 32.1	13 05

Figure 8–1. **Typical daily page from the *Nautical Almanac* showing the astronomical data for the 4 major planets and 57 navigational stars**

a practical example of a planet sight, following the six standard steps of the celestial process as before, and noting the minor procedural exceptions as we progress. As navigator, this time you are on an Atlantic crossing, and just after sunset on October 18, 1984, at DR position Latitude 41°04′N, Longitude 60°41′W, you make an observation of Venus at a sextant altitude of 12°29.9′. Your watch reads 21:20:03 GMT, and has no error; the index correction is –2.4′, and the height of eye, 9 feet. The workform for planet sights is similar to those you have worked with in the earlier exercises. Completed for this example, and to be used to follow the explanation, the workbook looks like this:

DATE	Oct. 18, 1984
BODY	Venus
hs	12-29.9
IC	-2.4
D	-2.9
ha	12-24.6
R	-4.3
add'l corr	+0.1
Ho	12-20.4
W	21-20-03
corr	00
GMT	21-20-03
gha [v]	106-39.1 [-0.7]
incr	5-00.8
v corr	-0.2
GHA	111-39.7
aλ	60-39.7
LHA	51
dec [d]	20-41.1 [0.[illegible]] S
d corr	+0.3
Dec	20-41.4
a L	41 N
Tab Hc	12-49
corr	-33
Hc	12-16.0
Ho	12-20.4
a	4.4 T
Zn	228°

The first exception that applies to planet sights is the most important. In observing planets with your sextant, you must be sure to bring the *center* of the body to the horizon. Unlike stars, which show only a pinpoint of light, planets exhibit a visible disc when viewed through a magnifying eyepiece, and for accurate sights, it is essential that the center of the body, and not one of its limbs, be bisected by the horizon. The index correction and the correction for height of eye are found and applied in the same way as for other sights. Using our IC of –2.4′, and the correction of –2.9′ found in the dip table (Figure 8–2), the apparent altitude of Venus becomes 12°24.6′. The R-correction is then obtained from the PLANETS columns

STARS AND PLANETS

App. Alt.	Corrn
° ′	′
9 56	
	–5·3
10 08	
	–5·2
10 20	
	–5·1
10 33	
	–5·0
10 46	
	–4·9
11 00	
	–4·8
11 14	
	–4·7
11 29	
	–4·6
11 45	
	–4·5
12 01	
	–4·4
12 18	
	–4·3
12 35	
	–4·2
12 54	

App. Alt.	Additional Corrn
1984	
VENUS	
Jan. 1-Dec. 12	
°	′
0	+ 0·1
60	
Dec. 13-Dec. 31	
°	′
0	+ 0·2
41	+ 0·1
76	

DIP

Ht. of Eye	Corrn	Ht. of Eye
m	′	ft.
2·4		8·0
	–2·8	
2·6		8·6
	–2·9	
2·8		9·2
	–3·0	
3·0		9·8
	–3·1	
3·2		10·5
	–3·2	
3·4		11·2
	–3·3	
3·6		11·9
	–3·4	
3·8		12·6
	–3·5	
4·0		13·3
	–3·6	
4·3		14·1
	–3·7	
4·5		14·9
	–3·8	
4·7		15·7
	–3·9	
5·0		16·5

Ht. of Eye	Corrn
m	′
1·0	– 1·8
1·5	– 2·2
2·0	– 2·5
2·5	– 2·8
3·0	– 3·0
See table ←	
m	′
20	– 7·9
22	– 8·3
24	– 8·6
26	– 9·0

Figure 8–2. **Portion of the *Nautical Almanac*'s Altitude Correction Tables for stars and planets. The dip correction is –2.9′ for a 9-foot height of eye; the R-correction for Venus's apparent altitude of 12°24.6′ is –4.3′; there is an additional correction for Venus, +0.1′, for the date of the observation.**

of the altitude correction tables inside the front cover of the *Nautical Almanac*, which are excerpted in Figure 8–2. For an ha of 12°24.6′, the R-correction is –4.3′; for both planets and stars, it is always negative. In the case of certain planets, usually Venus and Mars, there may be a small additional correction like the one shown for Venus in Figure 8–2 of +0.1′. Applying both of these corrections to the apparent altitude, we arrive at the observed altitude, Ho, of 12°20.4′.

The Greenwich hour angle and the declination for our sight are taken from the almanac's daily page, shown in Figure 8–1. Figure 8–3 is a portion of this page covering

1984 OCTOBER 18, 19, 20

G.M.T.		ARIES	VENUS −3.4		MARS +0.6	
d	h	G.H.A. ° ′	G.H.A. ° ′	Dec. ° ′	G.H.A. ° ′	Dec. ° ′
18	00	26 39.8	151 53.2	S20 24.2	106 47.4	S25 08.9
	01	41 42.3	166 52.6	25.0	121 47.9	08.7
	02	56 44.8	181 51.9	25.8	136 48.4	08.6
	03	71 47.2	196 51.2	·· 26.6	151 48.9	·· 08.4
	04	86 49.7	211 50.6	27.4	166 49.4	08.3
	05	101 52.2	226 49.9	28.2	181 49.9	08.1
	06	116 54.6	241 49.2	S20 29.0	196 50.4	S25 08.0
	07	131 57.1	256 48.6	29.9	211 50.9	07.8
T	08	146 59.5	271 47.9	30.7	226 51.4	07.7
H	09	162 02.0	286 47.2	·· 31.5	241 51.9	·· 07.5
U	10	177 04.5	301 46.5	32.3	256 52.4	07.4
R	11	192 06.9	316 45.9	33.1	271 52.9	07.2
S	12	207 09.4	331 45.2	S20 33.9	286 53.4	S25 07.1
D	13	222 11.9	346 44.5	34.7	301 53.9	06.9
A	14	237 14.3	1 43.8	35.5	316 54.4	06.8
Y	15	252 16.8	16 43.2	·· 36.3	331 54.9	·· 06.6
	16	267 19.3	31 42.5	37.1	346 55.4	06.5
	17	282 21.7	46 41.8	37.9	1 55.9	06.3
	18	297 24.2	61 41.1	S20 38.7	16 56.4	S25 06.1
	19	312 26.6	76 40.5	39.5	31 56.9	06.0
	20	327 29.1	91 39.8	40.3	46 57.4	05.8
	21	342 31.6	106 39.1	·· 41.1	61 57.9	·· 05.7
	22	357 34.0	121 38.4	41.9	76 58.4	05.5
	23	12 36.5	136 37.7	42.7	91 58.9	05.4
Mer. Pass.		h m 22 05.8	*v* −0.7	*d* 0.8	*v* 0.5	*d* 0.2

Figure 8–3. **Excerpt from the *Nautical Almanac* showing the astronomical data for Venus on October 18, 1984. At 21ʰ GMT, Venus's GHA is 106°39.1′, and the Dec 20°41.1′S. Note the *v* and *d* values at the bottom of the table, which apply for the entire day.**

the particular data we need. You will note that the tabulations are similar to those for the sun and moon, except that the values of v and d are given only at the bottom of the table, and apply for the whole day. For our sight, the GHA of Venus at 21 hours GMT is seen to be 106°39.1′, with a v of –0.7′. The tabular declination at the same hour is 20°41.1′S, and the value of d is 0.8′; positive, because the declination is increasing. The corrections to the tabular Greenwich hour angle are found, as usual, in the tables in the back of the almanac; an excerpt for 20 minutes of time is seen in Figure 8–4. Be sure to use the PLANETS column, which is shared with the sun, and to extract the v- and d-corrections at the same time. For our example, the GHA increment for 20ᵐ03ˢ is 5°00.8′, and the v-correction, –0.2′ (remember that the v-value was negative in this case). Applying the hour-angle correc-

20ᵐ INCREMENTS AND CORRECTIONS

ᵐ 20	SUN PLANETS	ARIES	MOON	v or d	Corrⁿ	v or d	Corrⁿ	v or d	Corrⁿ
s	° ′	° ′	° ′	′	′	′	′	′	′
00	5 00·0	5 00·8	4 46·3	0·0	0·0	6·0	2·1	12·0	4·1
01	5 00·3	5 01·1	4 46·6	0·1	0·0	6·1	2·1	12·1	4·1
02	5 00·5	5 01·3	4 46·8	0·2	0·1	6·2	2·1	12·2	4·2
03	5 00·8	5 01·6	4 47·0	0·3	0·1	6·3	2·2	12·3	4·2
04	5 01·0	5 01·8	4 47·3	0·4	0·1	6·4	2·2	12·4	4·2
05	5 01·3	5 02·1	4 47·5	0·5	0·2	6·5	2·2	12·5	4·3
06	5 01·5	5 02·3	4 47·8	0·6	0·2	6·6	2·3	12·6	4·3
07	5 01·8	5 02·6	4 48·0	0·7	0·2	6·7	2·3	12·7	4·3
08	5 02·0	5 02·8	4 48·2	0·8	0·3	6·8	2·3	12·8	4·4
09	5 02·3	5 03·1	4 48·5	0·9	0·3	6·9	2·4	12·9	4·4

Figure 8–4. **Excerpt from the *Increments and Corrections* tables showing the GHA increment for 20ᵐ03ˢ, and the appropriate *v*- and *d*-corrections**

tions to the tabular value, Venus's final GHA becomes 111°39.7′. The *d*-correction amounts to 0.3′, and that added to the tabular dec produces a declination of 20° 41.1′S.

By now you will have selected an assumed longitude of 60°39.7′W, near your DR position, and suitable for making the local hour angle a whole number. The selection of an assumed latitude at 41°N is equally obvious if you remember that we want the whole degree nearest our DR. The remainder of the procedure for reducing your planet sight follows the same routine you learned for the sun and the moon. The appropriate page of the sight reduction table, Pub. No. 249, is entered with the assumed latitude, 41°, the local hour angle, 51°, and the degrees of declination, 20°. The excerpt in Figure 8–5 is from the page that includes Venus's calculated declination, with its name contrary to that of the latitude; the declination in our example is South, and the assumed latitude North. From the table, opposite LHA 51°, and under declination 20°, we extract the tabular Hc of 12°49′, the altitude differential, *d*, of –48′, and the azimuth angle, Z, 132°. Note that *d* in this instance bears no relation to the *d* representing hourly change which we used in figuring the declination; don't be confused, they are entirely separate. The tabular Hc is corrected with Table 5 (Figure 8–6) in the regular way. For a *d* of –48, and minutes of declination of 41.4, the adjustment amounts to –33′, resulting in a final computed altitude, Hc, of 12° 16.0′. Comparing this with the previously calculated Ho, the intercept works out to 4.4′, "toward," because Ho is greater.

The rule for finding true azimuth is in the corner of the sight reduction table. With an LHA less than 180° (ours is 51°), Zn = 360° – Z, so our true azimuth for plotting, which is done in exactly the same way as for your other sights, is 228°. We turn now to the last category of celestial bodies, the stars.

N. Lat. {LHA greater than 180°........ Zn=Z; LHA less than 180°..........Zn=360—Z

LAT 41° DECLINATION (15°-29°) CONTRARY NAME TO LATITUDE

LHA	15° Hc	d	Z	16° Hc	d	Z	17° Hc	d	Z	18° Hc	d	Z	19° Hc	d	Z	20° Hc	d	Z
	° ′	′	°	° ′	′	°	° ′	′	°	° ′	′	°	° ′	′	°	° ′	′	°
69	05 15	43	115	04 32	42	116	03 50	43	117	03 07	42	117	02 25	43	118	01 42	42	119
68	05 56	43	116	05 13	43	117	04 30	42	117	03 48	43	118	03 05	43	119	02 22	43	119
67	06 36	43	117	05 53	42	117	05 11	44	118	04 27	43	119	03 44	43	119	03 01	43	120
66	07 17	43	117	06 34	44	118	05 50	43	119	05 07	43	119	04 24	44	120	03 40	43	121
65	07 57	−43	118	07 14	−44	119	06 30	−43	119	05 47	−44	120	05 03	−44	121	04 19	−43	121
64	08 37	44	119	07 53	44	119	07 09	43	120	06 26	44	121	05 42	44	121	04 58	44	122
63	09 16	43	119	08 33	44	120	07 49	45	121	07 04	44	121	06 20	44	122	05 36	44	123
62	09 56	44	120	09 12	45	121	08 27	44	121	07 43	45	122	06 58	44	123	06 14	45	123
61	10 35	45	121	09 50	44	121	09 06	45	122	08 21	45	123	07 36	44	124	06 52	45	124
60	11 14	−45	122	10 29	−45	122	09 44	−45	123	08 59	−45	124	08 14	−45	124	07 29	−45	125
59	11 52	45	122	11 07	45	123	10 22	45	124	09 37	46	124	08 51	45	125	08 06	45	126
58	12 30	45	123	11 45	46	124	10 59	45	124	10 14	46	125	09 28	45	126	08 43	46	126
57	13 08	46	124	12 22	45	124	11 37	46	125	10 51	46	126	10 05	46	126	09 19	46	127
56	13 46	46	125	13 00	46	125	12 14	47	126	11 27	46	126	10 41	46	127	09 55	46	128
55	14 23	−46	125	13 37	−47	126	12 50	−46	127	12 04	−47	127	11 17	−46	128	10 31	−47	129
54	15 00	47	126	14 13	47	127	13 26	46	127	12 40	47	128	11 53	47	129	11 06	47	129
53	15 36	47	127	14 49	47	127	14 02	47	128	13 15	47	129	12 28	47	129	11 41	48	130
52	16 12	47	128	15 25	47	128	14 38	48	129	13 50	47	130	13 03	48	130	12 15	47	131
51	16 48	48	128	16 00	47	129	15 13	48	130	14 25	48	130	13 37	48	131	12 49	48	132
50	17 23	−48	129	16 35	−48	130	15 47	−48	130	14 59	−48	131	14 11	−48	132	13 23	−48	132
49	17 58	48	130	17 10	48	131	16 22	49	131	15 33	48	132	14 45	49	132	13 56	48	133
48	18 33	49	131	17 44	48	131	16 56	49	132	16 07	49	133	15 18	49	133	14 29	49	134
47	19 07	49	132	18 18	49	132	17 29	49	133	16 40	49	133	15 51	49	134	15 02	50	135

LHA	21° Hc	d	Z	22° Hc	d	Z	23° Hc	d	Z	24° Hc	d	Z	25° Hc	d	Z	Hc
	° ′	′	°	° ′	′	°	° ′	′	°	° ′	′	°	° ′	′	°	°
69	01 00	43	119	00 17	42	120	−0 25	43	121	−1 08	43	121	−1 51	42	122	−2 3
68	01 39	43	120	00 56	43	121	00 13	42	121	−0 29	43	122	−1 12	43	123	−1 5
67	02 18	43	121	01 35	43	121	00 52	43	122	00 09	43	123	−0 34	44	123	−1 1
66	02 57	43	121	02 14	44	122	01 30	43	123	00 47	44	123	00 03	43	124	−0 4
65	03 36	−44	122	02 52	−44	123	02 08	−44	123	01 24	−43	124	00 41	−44	125	−0 0
64	04 14	44	123	03 30	44	123	02 46	44	124	02 02	44	125	01 18	44	125	00 3
63	04 52	45	123	04 07	44	124	03 23	44	125	02 39	45	125	01 54	44	126	01 1
62	05 29	44	124	04 45	45	125	04 00	44	125	03 16	45	126	02 31	45	127	01 4
61	06 07	45	125	05 22	45	126	04 37	45	126	03 52	45	127	03 07	45	127	02 2
60	06 44	−45	126	05 59	−46	126	05 13	−45	127	04 28	−45	127	03 43	−46	128	02 5
59	07 21	46	126	06 35	46	127	05 49	45	128	05 04	46	128	04 18	46	129	03 3
58	07 57	46	127	07 11	46	128	06 25	46	128	05 39	46	129	04 53	46	130	04 0
57	08 33	46	128	07 47	46	128	07 01	47	129	06 14	46	130	05 28	46	130	04 4
56	09 09	47	128	08 22	46	129	07 36	47	130	06 49	47	130	06 02	46	131	05 1
55	09 44	−47	129	08 57	−47	130	08 10	−47	130	07 23	−47	131	06 36	−47	132	05 4
54	10 19	47	130	09 32	47	131	08 45	48	131	07 57	47	132	07 10	47	132	06 2
53	10 53	47	131	10 06	47	131	09 19	48	132	08 31	48	133	07 43	47	133	06 5
52	11 28	48	131	10 40	48	132	09 52	48	133	09 04	48	133	08 16	48	134	07 2
51	12 01	48	132	11 13	48	133	10 25	48	133	09 37	48	134	08 49	49	135	08 0
50	12 35	−49	133	11 46	−48	134	10 58	−49	134	10 09	−48	135	09 21	−49	135	08 3
49	13 08	49	134	12 19	49	134	11 30	49	135	10 41	49	135	09 52	48	136	09 0
48	13 40	49	134	12 51	49	135	12 02	49	136	11 13	49	136	10 24	50	137	09 3
47	14 12	49	135	13 23	49	136	12 34	50	136	11 44	50	137	10 54	49	138	10 0

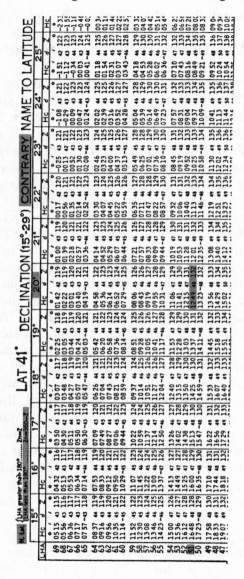

Figure 8–5. **Excerpt from Pub. No. 249, Volume III, showing the values for Latitude 41°N, Declination 20°S, and LHA 51° to be: Hc 12°49′, *d* –48′, Z 132°**

43	44	45	46	47	48	49	50	51	52	53	54	55	56	57	58	59	60	d ′
0	0	0	0	0	0	0	0	0	0	0	0	0	0	0	0	0	0	0
1	1	1	1	1	1	1	1	1	1	1	1	1	1	1	1	1	1	1
1	1	2	2	2	2	2	2	2	2	2	2	2	2	2	2	2	2	2
2	2	2	2	2	2	2	2	3	3	3	3	3	3	3	3	3	3	3
3	3	3	3	3	3	3	3	3	3	4	4	4	4	4	4	4	4	4
4	4	4	4	4	4	4	4	4	4	4	4	5	5	5	5	5	5	5
4	4	4	5	5	5	5	5	5	5	5	5	6	6	6	6	6	6	6
5	5	5	5	5	6	6	6	6	6	6	6	6	7	7	7	7	7	7
6	6	6	6	6	6	7	7	7	7	7	7	7	7	8	8	8	8	8
6	7	7	7	7	7	7	8	8	8	8	8	8	8	9	9	9	9	9
7	7	8	8	8	8	8	8	8	9	9	9	9	9	10	10	10	10	10
8	8	8	8	9	9	9	9	9	10	10	10	10	10	10	11	11	11	11
9	9	9	9	9	10	10	10	10	10	11	11	11	11	11	12	12	12	12
9	10	10	10	10	10	11	11	11	11	11	12	12	12	12	13	13	13	13
10	10	10	11	11	11	11	12	12	12	12	13	13	13	13	14	14	14	14
11	11	11	12	12	12	12	12	13	13	13	14	14	14	14	14	15	15	15
11	12	12	12	13	13	13	13	14	14	14	14	15	15	15	15	16	16	16
12	12	13	13	13	14	14	14	14	15	15	15	16	16	16	16	17	17	17
13	13	14	14	14	14	15	15	15	16	16	16	16	17	17	17	18	18	18
14	14	14	15	15	15	16	16	16	16	17	17	17	18	18	18	19	19	19
14	15	15	15	16	16	16	17	17	17	18	18	18	19	19	19	20	20	20
15	15	16	16	16	17	17	18	18	18	19	19	19	20	20	20	21	21	21
16	16	16	17	17	18	18	18	19	19	19	20	20	21	21	21	22	22	22
16	17	17	18	18	18	19	19	20	20	20	21	21	21	22	22	23	23	23
17	18	18	18	19	19	20	20	20	21	21	22	22	22	23	23	24	24	24
18	18	19	19	20	20	20	21	21	22	22	22	23	23	24	24	25	25	25
19	19	20	20	20	21	21	22	22	23	23	23	24	24	25	25	26	26	26
19	20	20	21	21	22	22	22	23	23	24	24	25	25	26	26	27	27	27
20	21	21	21	22	22	23	23	24	24	25	25	26	26	27	27	28	28	28
21	21	22	22	23	23	24	24	25	25	26	26	27	27	28	28	29	29	29
22	22	22	23	24	24	24	25	26	26	26	27	28	28	28	29	30	30	30
22	23	23	24	24	25	25	26	26	27	27	28	28	29	29	30	30	31	31
23	23	24	25	25	26	26	27	27	28	28	29	29	30	30	31	31	32	32
24	24	25	25	26	26	27	28	28	29	29	30	30	31	31	32	32	33	33
24	25	26	26	27	27	28	28	29	29	30	31	31	32	32	33	33	34	34
25	26	26	27	27	28	29	29	30	30	31	32	32	33	33	34	34	35	35
26	26	27	28	28	29	29	30	31	31	32	32	33	34	34	35	35	36	36
27	27	28	28	29	30	30	31	31	32	33	33	34	35	35	36	36	37	37
27	28	28	29	30	30	31	32	32	33	34	34	35	35	36	37	37	38	38
28	29	29	30	31	31	32	32	33	34	34	35	36	36	37	38	38	39	39
29	29	30	31	31	32	33	33	34	35	35	36	37	37	38	39	39	40	40
29	30	31	31	32	33	33	34	35	36	36	37	38	38	39	40	40	41	41
30	31	32	32	33	34	34	35	36	36	37	38	38	39	40	41	41	42	42
31	32	32	33	34	34	35	36	37	37	38	39	39	40	41	42	42	43	43
32	32	33	34	34	35	36	37	37	38	39	40	40	41	42	43	43	44	44

Figure 8–6. **Excerpt from Table 5, Pub. No. 249, showing a correction of –33′ for *d* of –48′ and incremental minutes of declination, 41**

9 The Stars

Most laymen, when they think about celestial navigation, think first of the stars, but for experienced yacht navigators, this is not usually the case. Stars do offer the attractive possibility of being able to make observations of several of them within a short period of time, thus producing lines of position which can be crossed for a simultaneous fix, and certain stars are particularly easy to reduce with Volume I of Pub. No. 249. On the other hand, shooting the stars from the deck of a small boat is much more demanding than sights of the sun or moon, and the quality of the results is not as good. Let's talk about the easy part first—solving a star sight for its line of position—and follow that process by means of a practical example; then we will return to the special problems in making the actual sextant observation.

A navigator in DR position Latitude 40°53′N, Longitude 67°49′W, takes a sight of Arcturus during evening twilight on June 8, 1984. The sextant reads 63°03.2′, the index correction is –2.4′, and the height of eye, 9 feet. The watch is set to GMT, with no error, and reads 00:20:09, *June 9*, because the new day has already started in Greenwich. (This is a point to look out for in evening sights in west longitudes; be sure you have Greenwich mean time on the right day.)

The six standard steps which you have followed with all the other celestial bodies apply equally to the stars, but when you come to the sight reduction step, you have a choice between the volumes of Pub. No. 249. To illustrate the procedure and your two options, the respective workforms, completed for our practical example, are displayed here in parallel. We will discuss the differences, which first appear at the almanac step, as we proceed.

Stars—Vol. I Pub. No. 249

DATE	June 9, 1984
BODY	Arcturus
hs	63-03.2
IC	-2.4
D	-2.9
ha	62-57.9
R	-0.5
Ho	62-57.4
W	00-20-09
corr	00
GMT	00-20-09
gha ♈	257-32.6
incr	5-03.1
GHA ♈	262-35.7
aλ	67-35.7
LHA ♈	195
a L	41 N
Hc	63-01.0
Ho	62-57.4
a	3.6A
Zn	138°

Stars—Vol. II/III Pub. No. 249

DATE	June 9, 1984
BODY	Arcturus
hs	63-03.2
IC	-2.4
D	-2.9
ha	62-57.9
R	-0.5
Ho	62-57.4
W	00-20-09
corr	00
GMT	00-20-09
gha ♈	257-32.6
incr	5-03.1
GHA ♈	262-35.7
SHA★	146-15.7
	-360
GHA★	48-51.4
	+360
	408-51.4
a λ	67-51.4
LHA★	341
Dec	19-15.9 N
a L	41 N
Tab Hc	62-40
corr	+13
Hc	62-53.0
Ho	62-57.4
a	4.4T
Zn	138°

The sextant observation of a star is similar to that of a planet; the point-source of light should appear to bisect the horizon. Corrections for index error and dip are made in the usual way, and the refraction, or R-correction, is taken from the STARS column of the almanac's altitude correction tables, Figure 9–1. In our example, the index correction of –2.4′, and the –2.9′-dip correction, found in the dip table for the 9-foot height of eye, are applied to the sextant altitude of 63°03.2′ to produce the apparent altitude, 62°57.9′. Entering the STARS column of Figure 9–1, the R-correction for the apparent altitude we calculated is –0.5′. For the stars there is always just a single R-correc-

STARS AND PLANETS

App. Alt.	Corrn	App. Alt.	Additional Corrn
° ′	′		
9 56			**1984**
	−5·3		**VENUS**
10 08			Jan. 1-Dec. 12
	−5·2		
10 20			
	−5·1		
10 33		°	′
	−5·0		
10 46		0	+ 0·1
52 18			
	−0·7		
56 11			
	−0·6		
60 28			
	−0·5		
65 08			
	−0·4		
70 11			
	−0·3		
75 34			
	−0·2		
81 13			
	−0·1		
87 03			
	0·0		
90 00			

DIP

Ht. of Eye	Corrn	Ht. of Eye	Ht. of Eye	Corrn
m		ft.	m	′
2·4	′	8·0	1·0	− 1·8
	−2·8			
2·6		8·6	1·5	− 2·2
	−2·9			
2·8		9·2	2·0	− 2·5
	−3·0			
3·0		9·8	2·5	− 2·8
	−3·1			
3·2		10·5	3·0	− 3·0
17·4		57·4	120	− 10·6
	−7·4			
17·9		58·9	125	− 10·8
	−7·5			
18·4		60·5		
	−7·6			
18·8		62·1	130	− 11·1
	−7·7			
19·3		63·8	135	− 11·3
	−7·8			
19·8		65·4	140	− 11·5
	−7·9			
20·4		67·1	145	− 11·7
	−8·0			
20·9		68·8	150	− 11·9
	−8·1			
21·4		70·5	155	− 12·1

Figure 9–1. **Portion of Altitude Correction Tables from the *Nautical Almanac* showing the dip correction of –2.9′ for a height of eye of 9 feet, and the star's refraction correction of –0.5′ for an apparent altitude of 62°57.9′**

tion, and as it is for the planets, the correction is always negative. When the R-correction is applied in our exercise, the observed altitude, Ho, of Arcturus becomes 62° 57.4′. Timing a star sight is also identical to timing any other celestial observation; just be sure, as we have mentioned, that you have identified the correct Greenwich day. In our practical example, the time was 00:20:09, after midnight in Greenwich although it was only evening, local time, in the longitude where the observation was made.

In the third step, obtaining the astronomical data from the almanac, you will see a slight difference in star sights in the process of determining the Greenwich hour angle from the almanac's daily pages. Figure 8–1 illustrates a typical left-hand daily page from the *Nautical Almanac.* It is called the "star side," because it contains all the information for the 57 navigational stars as well as the planet data. An excerpt of the page covering our observation of Arcturus is shown in Figure 9–2. Since the stars change position with respect to each other only at a very slow rate, the almanac designers, in order to simply the presentation, have chosen to show the data for an arbitrary, single point on the celestial sphere, and relate all the stars' positions to it. The arbitrary point, which is called the First Point of Aries, or Vernal Equinox, and is indicated by the symbol, ♈, is tabulated in the almanac as if it were a celestial body. All the stars are positioned from Aries by their sidereal hour angle, a measurement similar to Greenwich hour angle, but reckoned westward from the First Point of Aries instead of from Greenwich. Thus the simple formula:

$$\text{GHA Aries} + \text{SHA star} = \text{GHA star}$$

Returning to our practical example, from the ARIES column in the almanac excerpt in Figure 9–2, you will

1984 JUNE 8, 9, 10

G.M.T. d	G.M.T. h	ARIES G.H.A. ° ′
8	00	256 33.5
	01	271 36.0
	02	286 38.4
	03	301 40.9
	04	316 43.4
	05	331 45.8
	06	346 48.3
	07	1 50.7
	08	16 53.2
F	09	31 55.7
R	10	46 58.1
I	11	62 00.6
D	12	77 03.1
A	13	92 05.5
Y	14	107 08.0
	15	122 10.5
	16	137 12.9
	17	152 15.4
	18	167 17.9
	19	182 20.3
	20	197 22.8
	21	212 25.2
	22	227 27.7
	23	242 30.2
9	00	257 32.6
	01	272 35.1
	02	287 37.6

STARS Name	S.H.A. ° ′	Dec. ° ′
Acamar	315 35.5	S40 21.9
Achernar	335 43.4	S57 18.8
Acrux	173 34.2	S63 01.0
Adhara	255 30.3	S28 57.0
Aldebaran	291 15.2	N16 28.7
Alioth	166 39.7	N56 03.0
Alkaid	153 15.9	N49 23.7
Al Na'ir	28 11.2	S47 02.1
Alnilam	276 09.2	S 1 12.6
Alphard	218 18.1	S 8 35.4
Alphecca	126 29.4	N26 46.1
Alpheratz	358 06.7	N29 00.0
Altair	62 29.6	N 8 49.4
Ankaa	353 37.6	S42 23.3
Antares	112 53.2	S26 24.0
Arcturus	146 15.7	N19 15.9
Atria	108 14.5	S69 00.1
Avior	234 27.7	S59 27.7
Bellatrix	278 56.2	N 6 20.2
Betelgeuse	271 25.7	N 7 24.3
Canopus	264 06.6	S52 41.2
Capella	281 07.8	N45 59.0
Deneb	49 46.4	N45 13.1

***Figure 9–2.* Extract from the *Nautical Almanac* daily page showing the astronomical data for the star Arcturus on June 9 at 00^h GMT**

see that the GHA ♈ at 00 hours on June 9, is 257°32.6′. The incremental minutes and seconds of time are dealt with in the *Increments and Corrections* tables, Figure 9–3, in the usual manner, making certain that you use only the ARIES column. The tabular Greenwich hour angle of Aries (257°32.6′) plus the increment, of 5°03.1′ for the 20 minutes and 09 seconds of time, produce the GHA ,
shown on the workforms to be 262°35.7′.

Having found Aries's Greenwich hour angle, you now have the choice of volumes mentioned earlier. The first

m 20	SUN PLANETS	ARIES	MOON	v or d	Corrⁿ	v or d	Corrⁿ	v or d	Corrⁿ
s	° ′	° ′	° ′	′	′	′	′	′	′
00	5 00·0	5 00·8	4 46·3	0·0	0·0	6·0	2·1	12·0	4·1
01	5 00·3	5 01·1	4 46·6	0·1	0·0	6·1	2·1	12·1	4·1
02	5 00·5	5 01·3	4 46·8	0·2	0·1	6·2	2·1	12·2	4·2
03	5 00·8	5 01·6	4 47·0	0·3	0·1	6·3	2·2	12·3	4·2
04	5 01·0	5 01·8	4 47·3	0·4	0·1	6·4	2·2	12·4	4·2
05	5 01·3	5 02·1	4 47·5	0·5	0·2	6·5	2·2	12·5	4·3
06	5 01·5	5 02·3	4 47·8	0·6	0·2	6·6	2·3	12·6	4·3
07	5 01·8	5 02·6	4 48·0	0·7	0·2	6·7	2·3	12·7	4·3
08	5 02·0	5 02·8	4 48·2	0·8	0·3	6·8	2·3	12·8	4·4
09	5 02·3	5 03·1	4 48·5	0·9	0·3	6·9	2·4	12·9	4·4
10	5 02·5	5 03·3	4 48·7	1·0	0·3	7·0	2·4	13·0	4·4
11	[illegible]	[illegible]	[illegible]	[illegible]	[illegible]	[illegible]	[illegible]	[illegible]	[illegible]

Figure 9–3. **Excerpt from the *Increments and Corrections* tables, showing an increment of 5°03.1′ to Aries's GHA for 20 minutes, 09 seconds of time**

and simplest is Volume I of Pub. No. 249, provided you have selected one of the seven stars listed for your local hour angle. It is quite likely that your star will be one appearing in the table, since you probably will have chosen it in advance for that very reason. On the other hand, if the declination of any star observed is less than 30°, you may elect to work the sight by Volume II or III, in the same way as for all the bodies of the solar system. To put the choice in perspective, of the 57 navigational stars listed in the almanac's daily pages, 7 stars are selected in Volume I for each degree of LHA♈; 41 are used altogether. Thirty of the 57 navigational stars, including seven of the lesser ones which do not appear in Volume I, can be worked with Volumes II or III. Thus, only 9, and those all minor stars, cannot be reduced with one or the other of the volumes of Pub. No. 249. Never, in my experience, has this been of consequence in the choice of Pub. No. 249 as the sight reduction table for yachtsmen.

With normal preplanning, you will probably use Volume I for most of your star sights, but since an even dozen of the 19 first-magnitude (brightest) stars in the almanac list can be worked with either volume, it is worthwhile to understand the procedure for each.

Looking first at Volume I, you will notice in the specimen page shown in Figure 9–4 a somewhat different arrangement from the Volume III reduction table page illustrated in Figure 4–1. Volume I requires only the latitude, the local hour angle of Aries, and the name of the star as entering arguments; the computed altitude, with no need for correction, and the true azimuth are read out directly. You don't have to concern yourself with the star's declination, or whether it is the same or contrary to the name of the latitude; you don't have to calculate the local hour angle of the star; you don't have to adjust the computed altitude for fractional degrees of declination; you don't have to convert azimuth angle to true azimuth; and it's all done with a single opening of the book.

Let's complete our practical example, which you can follow in the shorter of the workforms, using Volume I. Starting with the Greenwich hour angle of Aries, the assumed longitude is applied in the usual manner to obtain the local hour angle of Aries; here, an $a\lambda$ of 67° 35.7′W, applied to the GHA ♈ of 262°35.7′, produces an LHA ♈ of 195°. The assumed latitude is selected as for any sight, and Volume I opened to the corresponding page. The latitude assumed for our sight should be 41°N, the whole degree nearest to our DR latitude of 40°53′N. An excerpt of the appropriate page from Volume I appears in Figure 9–5. Descend the leftmost column to the LHA ♈ of the sight, 195°, and opposite it, under the name of the

***Figure 9–4.* Specimen page from Volume I *(Selected Stars),* Pub. No. 249, Epoch 1985.0. Only latitude, LHA ♈, and the name of the star are required to obtain Hc and Zn directly**

1°N

Zn	Hc	Zn	Hc	Zn	Hc	Zn	Hc	Zn	Hc	Zn	Hc	Zn
ab	•VEGA		ARCTURUS		•SPICA		REGULUS		•POLLUX		CAPELLA	
017	18 31	054	53 59	117	34 24	155	52 00	228	36 59	277	21 46	313
017	19 08	055	54 39	118	34 43	156	51 25	230	36 14	278	21 13	313
017	19 45	055	55 19	119	35 01	157	50 50	231	35 29	278	20 40	314
016	20 23	056	55 58	120	35 18	158	50 15	232	34 45	279	20 07	314
016	21 00	056	56 37	122	35 35	159	49 39	233	34 00	280	19 35	315
016	21 38	057	57 15	123	35 50	160	49 02	235	33 15	280	19 03	315
016	22 16	057	57 53	124	36 05	162	48 25	236	32 31	281	18 31	316
015	22 54	058	58 30	126	36 19	163	47 47	237	31 46	281	17 59	316
015	23 33	058	59 07	127	36 32	164	47 09	238	31 02	282	17 28	317
015	24 11	059	59 42	128	36 44	165	46 31	239	30 18	282	16 57	317
014	24 50	059	60 18	130	36 55	166	45 52	240	29 34	283	16 26	317
014	25 29	060	60 52	131	37 05	168	45 12	241	28 49	283	15 56	318
014	26 08	060	61 25	133	37 15	169	44 32	242	28 05	284	15 26	318
013	26 48	061	61 58	135	37 23	170	43 52	243	27 22	285	14 56	319
013	27 27	061	62 30	136	37 30	171	43 12	244	26 38	285	14 26	319
A	Rasalhague		ARCTURUS		•SPICA		REGULUS		•POLLUX		Dubhe	
062	24 20	094	63 01	138	37 37	172	42 31	245	25 54	286	62 45	330
062	25 05	095	63 30	140	37 42	174	41 49	246	25 11	286	62 22	329
062	25 50	096	63 59	142	37 47	175	41 08	247	24 27	287	61 59	329
063	26 35	096	64 26	144	37 50	176	40 26	248	23 44	287	61 35	328
063	27 20	097	64 53	146	37 53	177	39 44	249	23 01	288	61 11	327
064	28 05	098	65 18	148	37 54	179	39 02	250	22 18	288	60 46	327
064	28 50	099	65 41	150	37 55	180	38 19	250	21 35	289	60 21	327
065	29 35	099	66 04	152	37 55	181	37 36	251	20 52	290	59 56	326
065	30 19	100	66 24	154	37 53	182	36 53	252	20 10	290	59 31	326
066	31 04	101	66 43	156	37 51	184	36 10	253	19 27	291	59 05	325
066	31 48	102	67 01	158	37 48	185	35 27	254	18 45	291	58 39	325
067	32 33	102	67 17	161	37 43	186	34 43	255	18 03	292	58 13	325
067	33 17	103	67 31	163	37 38	187	34 00	255	17 21	292	57 47	324
067	34 01	104	67 43	166	37 32	189	33 16	256	16 39	293	57 20	324
068	34 45	105	67 53	168	37 24	190	32 32	257	15 58	294	56 54	324
EB	VEGA		Rasalhague		ANTARES		•ARCTURUS		REGULUS		•Dubhe	
048	38 22	068	35 28	105	14 19	146	68 02	171	31 47	258	56 27	323
049	39 04	069	36 12	106	14 44	147	68 08	173	31 03	258	56 00	323
049	39 46	069	36 55	107	15 09	148	68 13	176	30 19	259	55 32	323
050	40 29	070	37 39	108	15 32	149	68 15	178	29 34	260	55 05	323
050	41 11	070	38 22	109	15 56	149	68 16	181	28 50	261	54 37	322
051	41 54	070	39 04	110	16 19	150	68 14	183	28 05	261	54 10	322
051	42 36	071	39 47	110	16 41	151	68 10	186	27 20	262	53 42	322
051	43 19	071	40 29	111	17 02	152	68 05	188	26 35	263	53 14	322
052	44 02	072	41 11	112	17 23	153	67 57	191	25 50	263	52 46	322
052	44 45	072	41 53	113	17 44	154	67 48	193	25 05	264	52 18	322
053	45 28	073	42 35	114	18 03	155	67 37	196	24 20	265	51 50	322
053	46 12	073	43 16	115	18 23	155	67 24	198	23 35	266	51 22	322
053	46 55	073	43 57	116	18 41	156	67 09	200	22 50	266	50 54	321
054	47 38	074	44 37	117	18 59	157	66 52	203	22 05	267	50 26	321
054	48 22	074	45 17	118	19 16	158	66 34	205	21 19	268	49 58	321
EB	•ALTAIR		Rasalhague		ANTARES		•ARCTURUS		Denebola		•Dubhe	
055	18 57	095	45 57	119	19 33	159	66 14	207	40 56	252	49 29	321
055	19 42	095	46 37	120	19 49	160	65 52	209	40 13	253	49 01	321
055	20 27	096	47 16	121	20 04	161	65 29	211	39 30	254	48 33	321
056	21 12	097	47 54	122	20 18	162	65 05	213	38 46	254	48 04	321
056	21 57	098	48 32	123	20 32	163	64 39	215	38 03	255	47 36	321
057	22 42	098	49 10	124	20 45	164	64 13	217	37 19	256	47 08	321
057	23 27	099	49 47	126	20 58	165	63 44	219	36 35	257	46 39	321
057	24 12	100	50 24	127	21 09	165	63 15	221	35 51	258	46 11	321
058	24 56	100	51 00	128	21 20	166	62 45	223	35 06	258	45 43	321
058	25 41	101	51 35	129	21 31	167	62 14	225	34 22	259	45 15	321
058	26 25	102	52 10	130	21 40	168	61 41	226	33 37	260	44 46	322
059	27 09	103	52 44	132	21 49	169	61 08	228	32 53	261	44 18	322
059	27 53	103	53 17	133	21 57	170	60 34	229	32 08	261	43 50	322
060	28 37	104	53 50	134	22 04	171	60 00	231	31 23	262	43 22	322
060	29 21	105	54 22	136	22 11	172	59 24	232	30 38	263	42 54	322
EB	ALTAIR		Rasalhague		•ANTARES		ARCTURUS		Denebola		•Dubhe	
060	30 05	106	54 53	137	22 17	173	58 48	234	29 53	264	42 26	322
061	30 48	106	55 23	139	22 22	174	58 11	235	29 08	264	41 58	322
061	31 32	107	55 53	140	22 26	175	57 34	236	28 23	265	41 31	322
061	32 15	108	56 21	142	22 30	176	56 56	238	27 38	266	41 03	322
062	32 58	109	56 49	143	22 32	177	56 17	239	26 53	266	40 35	323
062	33 41	110	57 15	145	22 34	178	55 38	240	26 08	267	40 08	323
062	34 23	110	57 41	147	22 36	179	54 59	241	25 22	268	39 40	323
062	35 06	111	58 05	148	22 36	180	54 19	243	24 37	268	39 13	323
063	35 48	112	58 28	150	22 36	181	53 38	244	23 52	269	38 46	323
063	36 30	113	58 51	152	22 35	182	52 57	245	23 07	270	38 19	323
063	37 11	114	59 11	153	22 33	183	52 16	246	22 21	270	37 52	323
064	37 52	115	59 31	155	22 30	184	51 35	247	21 36	271	37 25	324
064	38 33	116	59 49	157	22 27	185	50 53	248	20 51	272	36 58	324
064	39 14	117	60 06	159	22 23	186	50 11	249	20 06	272	36 31	324
065	39 54	118	60 22	161	22 18	187	49 29	250	19 20	273	36 05	324
EB	ALTAIR		Nunki		•ANTARES		ARCTURUS		•Alkaid		Kochab	
065	40 34	118	17 39	153	22 12	188	48 46	251	55 36	301	53 36	346
065	41 14	119	17 59	154	22 06	189	48 03	252	54 57	301	53 24	345
065	41 53	120	18 18	155	21 59	190	47 20	253	54 18	301	53 13	345
066	42 32	121	18 37	156	21 51	190	46 37	254	53 39	301	53 01	345
066	43 10	122	18 55	157	21 42	191	45 53	254	53 00	301	52 49	345
066	43 48	124	19 13	158	21 33	192	45 09	255	52 22	301	52 37	344
066	44 26	125	19 30	159	21 23	193	44 25	256	51 43	301	52 25	344
067	45 03	126	19 46	159	21 12	194	43 41	257	51 04	302	52 12	344
067	45 40	127	20 02	160	21 01	195	42 57	258	50 26	302	51 59	343
067	46 16	128	20 16	161	20 48	196	42 13	259	49 48	302	51 46	343
067	46 51	129	20 31	162	20 35	197	41 29	259	49 09	302	51 33	343
067	47 26	130	20 44	163	20 22	198	40 44	260	48 31	302	51 19	343
068	48 00	131	20 57	164	20 07	199	39 59	261	47 53	303	51 06	342
068	48 34	133	21 09	165	19 52	200	39 15	262	47 15	303	50 52	342
068	49 07	134	21 20	166	19 37	201	38 30	262	46 37	303	50 38	342

LAT 41°N

LHA ♈	Hc	Zn	Hc	Zn	Hc	Zn	Hc	Zn	Hc	Zn	Hc	Zn	Hc	Zn
	•Alpheratz		ALTAIR		Nunki		•ANTARES		ARCTURUS		•Alkaid		Kochab	
270	17 14	066	49 39	135	21 31	167	19 20	202	37 45	263	45 59	303	50 24	342
271	17 55	067	50 11	136	21 41	168	19 03	203	37 00	264	45 21	303	50 10	342
272	18 37	067	50 41	138	21 50	169	18 45	203	36 15	265	44 43	304	49 55	341
273	19 19	068	51 11	139	21 58	170	18 27	204	35 30	265	44 05	304	49 41	341
274	20 01	068	51 41	141	22 06	171	18 08	205	34 45	266	43 28	304	49 26	341
275	20 43	069	52 09	142	22 13	172	17 49	206	33 59	267	42 51	304	49 11	341
276	21 26	070	52 36	143	22 19	173	17 28	207	33 14	267	42 13	305	48 56	341
277	22 08	070	53 03	145	22 24	174	17 07	208	32 29	268	41 36	305	48 41	340
278	22 51	071	53 29	146	22 29	175	16 46	209	31 44	269	40 59	305	48 26	340
279	23 34	071	53 53	148	22 33	176	16 24	210	30 58	269	40 22	306	48 10	340
280	24 16	072	54 17	149	22 36	177	16 01	210	30 13	270	39 45	306	47 55	340
281	25 00	072	54 39	151	22 38	177	15 38	211	29 28	271	39 09	306	47 40	340
282	25 43	073	55 01	153	22 40	178	15 14	212	28 42	271	38 32	306	47 24	340
283	26 26	073	55 21	154	22 41	179	14 50	213	27 57	272	37 56	307	47 08	340
284	27 10	074	55 40	156	22 41	180	14 25	214	27 12	273	37 20	307	46 52	340
	•Mirfak		Alpheratz		•ALTAIR		Rasalhague		•ARCTURUS		Alkaid		Kochab	
285	12 29	032	27 53	075	55 58	158	55 56	220	26 27	273	36 43	307	46 37	339
286	12 54	033	28 37	075	56 15	159	55 27	221	25 42	274	36 08	308	46 21	339
287	13 18	033	29 21	076	56 30	161	54 57	223	24 56	274	35 32	308	46 05	339
288	13 43	034	30 05	076	56 44	163	54 26	224	24 11	275	34 56	308	45 49	339
289	14 09	034	30 49	077	56 57	164	53 54	225	23 26	276	34 21	309	45 33	339
290	14 35	035	31 33	077	57 09	166	53 21	227	22 41	276	33 45	309	45 16	339
291	15 01	035	32 17	078	57 19	168	52 48	228	21 56	277	33 10	309	45 00	339
292	15 27	036	33 01	078	57 28	170	52 14	229	21 11	278	32 35	310	44 44	339
293	15 54	036	33 46	079	57 35	172	51 39	231	20 26	278	32 01	310	44 28	339
294	16 21	037	34 30	080	57 41	173	51 04	232	19 42	279	31 26	310	44 12	339
295	16 48	037	35 15	080	57 45	175	50 28	233	18 57	279	30 52	311	43 55	339
296	17 16	038	35 59	081	57 48	177	49 51	234	18 12	280	30 17	311	43 39	339
297	17 44	038	36 44	081	57 49	179	49 14	235	17 28	281	29 43	311	43 23	339
298	18 12	039	37 29	082	57 50	181	48 37	237	16 43	281	29 09	312	43 06	339
299	18 40	039	38 14	082	57 48	183	47 59	238	15 59	282	28 36	312	42 50	339
	Mirfak		•Alpheratz		Enif		•ALTAIR		Rasalhague		Alphecca		•Kochab	
300	19 09	040	38 59	083	51 21	137	57 45	185	47 20	239	34 21	277	42 34	339
301	19 38	040	39 44	084	51 52	138	57 41	186	46 41	240	33 36	278	42 17	339
302	20 08	041	40 29	084	52 22	139	57 35	188	46 02	241	32 51	279	42 01	339
303	20 37	041	41 14	085	52 51	141	57 28	190	45 22	242	32 07	279	41 45	339
304	21 07	041	41 59	085	53 19	142	57 19	192	44 42	243	31 22	280	41 29	339
305	21 37	042	42 44	086	53 46	144	57 09	194	44 02	244	30 37	280	41 12	339
306	22 08	042	43 29	086	54 13	145	56 58	196	43 21	245	29 53	281	40 56	339
307	22 38	043	44 14	087	54 38	147	56 45	197	42 40	246	29 08	281	40 40	339
308	23 09	043	45 00	088	55 03	148	56 31	199	41 58	247	28 24	282	40 24	339
309	23 40	044	45 45	088	55 26	150	56 15	201	41 16	248	27 40	283	40 08	339
310	24 12	044	46 30	089	55 48	151	55 59	202	40 34	249	26 56	283	39 52	339
311	24 43	044	47 15	090	56 09	153	55 41	204	39 52	249	26 12	284	39 36	339
312	25 15	045	48 01	090	56 29	155	55 22	206	39 09	250	25 28	284	39 20	339
313	25 47	045	48 46	091	56 48	156	55 01	207	38 27	251	24 44	285	39 04	339
314	26 19	046	49 31	092	57 05	158	54 40	209	37 44	252	24 00	285	38 48	340
	CAPELLA		•Alpheratz		FOMALHAUT		•ALTAIR		Rasalhague		VEGA		•Kochab	
315	10 20	036	50 16	092	14 19	154	54 17	211	37 01	253	62 34	277	38 32	340
316	10 47	036	51 02	093	14 38	155	53 54	212	36 17	254	61 49	278	38 17	340
317	11 14	037	51 47	094	14 57	156	53 29	214	35 34	255	61 04	278	38 01	340
318	11 41	038	52 32	094	15 15	157	53 04	215	34 50	255	60 19	279	37 45	340
319	12 09	038	53 17	095	15 33	157	52 37	217	34 06	256	59 34	279	37 30	340
320	12 37	039	54 02	096	15 50	158	52 10	218	33 22	257	58 50	280	37 15	340
321	13 05	039	54 47	097	16 06	159	51 41	219	32 38	258	58 05	280	36 59	340
322	13 34	040	55 32	098	16 22	160	51 12	221	31 53	258	57 21	280	36 44	340
323	14 03	040	56 17	098	16 37	161	50 42	222	31 09	259	56 36	281	36 29	341
324	14 32	041	57 02	099	16 52	162	50 11	224	30 25	260	55 52	281	36 14	341
325	15 02	041	57 46	100	17 06	163	49 40	225	29 40	261	55 07	282	35 59	341
326	15 32	042	58 31	101	17 19	163	49 08	226	28 55	261	54 23	282	35 44	341
327	16 02	042	59 15	102	17 32	164	48 35	227	28 10	262	53 39	283	35 29	341
328	16 33	043	60 00	103	17 43	165	48 01	229	27 26	263	52 55	283	35 15	341
329	17 04	043	60 44	104	17 55	166	47 27	230	26 41	263	52 11	283	35 00	341
	•CAPELLA		Hamal		Diphda		•FOMALHAUT		ALTAIR		•VEGA		Kochab	
330	17 35	044	36 10	089	19 54	139	18 05	167	46 52	231	51 27	284	34 46	342
331	18 06	044	36 55	090	20 24	140	18 15	168	46 16	232	50 43	284	34 32	342
332	18 38	045	37 41	090	20 53	140	18 24	169	45 40	233	49 59	285	34 18	342
333	19 09	045	38 26	091	21 21	141	18 32	170	45 04	234	49 15	285	34 04	342
334	19 42	045	39 11	092	21 49	142	18 40	171	44 27	235	48 31	286	33 50	342
335	20 14	046	39 56	092	22 17	143	18 47	172	43 49	236	47 48	286	33 36	342
336	20 47	046	40 42	093	22 44	144	18 53	172	43 11	238	47 04	286	33 22	343
337	21 20	047	41 27	094	23 10	145	18 59	173	42 33	239	46 21	287	33 09	343
338	21 53	047	42 12	094	23 36	146	19 04	174	41 54	240	45 38	287	32 56	343
339	22 26	048	42 57	095	24 01	147	19 08	175	41 15	241	44 55	288	32 42	343
340	23 00	048	43 42	096	24 25	148	19 11	176	40 35	242	44 11	288	32 29	343
341	23 34	049	44 27	097	24 49	149	19 14	177	39 55	242	43 28	289	32 16	344
342	24 08	049	45 12	097	25 12	150	19 16	178	39 15	243	42 46	289	32 04	344
343	24 42	050	45 57	098	25 35	151	19 17	179	38 34	244	42 03	289	31 51	344
344	25 17	050	46 42	099	25 56	152	19 18	180	37 53	245	41 20	290	31 39	344
	•CAPELLA		ALDEBARAN		Diphda		•FOMALHAUT		ALTAIR		•VEGA		Kochab	
345	25 52	050	15 21	081	26 18	153	19 18	181	37 12	246	40 38	290	31 26	344
346	26 27	051	16 06	082	26 38	154	19 17	182	36 31	247	39 55	291	31 14	345
347	27 02	051	16 51	083	26 58	155	19 15	183	35 49	248	39 13	291	31 02	345
348	27 37	052	17 36	083	27 17	156	19 13	183	35 07	249	38 31	292	30 50	345
349	28 13	052	18 21	084	27 35	157	19 10	184	34 24	250	37 49	292	30 39	345
350	28 49	052	19 06	084	27 53	158	19 06	185	33 42	250	37 07	292	30 27	345
351	29 25	053	19 51	085	28 10	159	19 01	186	32 59	251	36 25	293	30 16	346
352	30 01	053	20 36	086	28 26	160	18 56	187	32 16	252	35 44	293	30 05	346
353	30 37	054	21 21	086	28 41	161	18 50	188	31 33	253	35 02	294	29 54	346
354	31 14	054	22 06	087	28 56	162	18 43	189	30 50	254	34 21	294	29 43	346
355	31 51	054	22 51	088	29 09	163	18 36	190	30 06	254	33 39	295	29 33	347
356	32 27	055	23 37	088	29 22	164	18 28	191	29 22	255	32 58	295	29 22	347
357	33 05	055	24 22	089	29 35	165	18 19	192	28 39	256	32 18	296	29 12	347
358	33 42	056	25 07	090	29 46	166	18 09	193	27 55	257	31 37	296	29 02	347
359	34 19	056	25 53	090	29 56	167	17 59	193	27 10	257	30 56	297	28 52	348

LAT 41°N

LHA ♈	Hc	Zn	Hc	Zn	Hc	Zn	Hc	Zn	Hc	Zn	Hc	Zn	Hc	Zn
	Kochab		•VEGA		ARCTURUS		•SPICA		REGULUS		•POLLUX		CAPELLA	
180	51 28	017	18 31	054	53 59	117	34 24	155	52 00	228	36 59	277	21 46	313
181	51 41	017	19 08	055	54 39	118	34 43	156	51 25	230	36 14	278	21 13	313
182	51 54	017	19 45	055	55 19	119	35 01	157	50 50	231	35 29	278	20 40	314
183	52 07	016	20 23	056	55 58	120	35 18	158	50 15	232	34 45	279	20 07	314
184	52 20	016	21 00	056	56 37	122	35 35	159	49 39	233	34 00	280	19 35	315
185	52 32	016	21 38	057	57 15	123	35 50	160	49 02	235	33 15	280	19 03	315
186	52 45	016	22 16	057	57 53	124	36 05	162	48 25	236	32 31	281	18 31	316
187	52 57	015	22 54	058	58 30	126	36 19	163	47 47	237	31 46	281	17 59	316
188	53 09	015	23 33	058	59 07	127	36 32	164	47 09	238	31 02	282	17 28	317
189	53 20	015	24 11	059	59 42	128	36 44	165	46 31	239	30 18	282	16 57	317
190	53 31	014	24 50	059	60 18	130	36 55	166	45 52	240	29 34	283	16 26	317
191	53 42	014	25 29	060	60 52	131	37 05	168	45 12	241	28 49	283	15 56	318
192	53 53	014	2[illegible] 08	060	61 25	133	37 15	169	44 32	242	28 05	284	15 26	318
193	54 04	013	26 48	061	61 58	135	37 23	170	43 52	243	27 22	285	14 56	319
194	54 14	013	27 27	061	62 30	136	37 30	171	43 12	244	26 38	285	14 26	319
	•VEGA		Rasalhague		ARCTURUS		•SPICA		REGULUS		•POLLUX		Dubhe	
195	28 07	062	24 20	094	63 01	138	37 37	172	42 31	245	25 54	286	62 45	330
196	28 47	062	25 05	095	63 30	140	37 42	174	41 49	246	25 11	286	62 22	329
197	29 27	062	25 50	096	63 59	142	37 47	175	41 08	247	24 27	287	61 59	329
198	30 07	063	26 35	096	64 26	144	37 50	176	40 26	248	23 44	287	61 35	328
199	30 47	063	27 20	097	64 53	146	37 53	177	39 44	249	23 01	288	61 11	327
200	31 28	064	28 05	098	65 18	148	37 54	179	39 02	250	22 18	288	60 46	327
201	32 09	064	28 50	099	65 41	150	37 55	180	38 19	250	21 35	289	60 21	327
202	[illegible]	[illegible]	[illegible]	[illegible]	[illegible]	[illegible]	[illegible]	[illegible]	[illegible]	[illegible]	[illegible]	[illegible]	[illegible]	[illegible]

Figure 9–5. **Excerpt from main tables of Volume I, Pub. No. 249 for Latitude 41°N. At LHA ♈ 195°, Arcturus's Hc is 63°01′, and Zn 138°.**

star, Arcturus, extract the computed altitude, 63°01′, and the true azimuth, 138°. The comparison between Hc and Ho is made in the usual way; in our example, it yields an intercept of 3.6′ to be plotted from the assumed position Latitude 41°N, Longitude 67°35.7′W, in the direction "away" from the true azimuth—the reciprocal of 138°. That is all there is to it.

While no corrections or interpolations are required with the figures from Volume I, you should notice that your copy of the table will be for a certain "epoch" year. The table used in our excerpts is for Epoch 1985.0, and the volume is updated every five years. If you are more than a year either side of the epoch year, you may wish to adjust your position line or fix, by means of Table 5 in the back of Volume I, for *precession* and *nutation*. These technical terms simply mean that while the stars' positions can be considered fixed for short periods, they do wander slowly over a period of years, and this should be taken into account. The majority of small-boat navigators ignore this correction, which only applies to sights worked with Volume I, but that can admit errors of two or three miles in the distant years, a matter of significance if you are counting on precise results.

If you choose to perform your star-sight reduction with Volumes II or III of Pub. No. 249, you can see the procedure outlined in the longer of the workforms, which has been completed for the same observation of Arcturus. After having established the Greenwich hour angle of Aries, 262°35.7′, you next calculate the Greenwich hour angle of the star. This is accomplished, in accordance with the formula described earlier, by adding the sidereal hour angle of the star to GHA Aries. The sidereal hour angle of Arcturus is found in the almanac list (Figure 9–2); for either June 8, 9, or 10, the SHA is 146°15.7′. That value is added to Aries's GHA (then subtracting 360° because the total exceeds 360°) to produce the Greenwich hour angle of Arcturus, 48°51.4′. At the same time that Arcturus's SHA is being taken from the almanac, you can also extract the declination—in this case, 19°15.9′N for use in the sight reduction table. Like the SHA, the declination of a star is changing so slowly that no correction is needed for any of the three days included on the same page. On the other hand, you may have noticed in the lower right-hand corner of the daily page (Figure 8–1), the sidereal hour angles of the principal planets. These values are only for 00 hours on the middle day of the three, and if you try to find the GHA of a planet by adding its sidereal hour angle to GHA Aries, a correction is necessary. It is much better to use the regular planet tables.

To the star's GHA, the assumed longitude must be applied to obtain the local hour angle of the star. In our example, we assumed a longitude of 67°51.4′W, near our DR longitude, and one which would allow the local hour angle to be a whole degree, 341°. Since the longitude assumed is greater than the star's Greenwich hour angle, 360° must first be added to the GHA to make the subtraction called for by the West longitude possible. You will notice in this particular case that in combining SHA★ with GHA♈, it was necessary to subtract 360°, and then, in the next step, when applying $a\lambda$ to GHA★, it was necessary to add it back again. By inspection, the navigator probably would have realized that by omitting the subtraction and later readdition of 360°, the result would have been the identical LHA★, and he might have skipped the extra steps which I included for clarity. You should also note that we used a somewhat different assumed longitude than we did in the Volume I solution; in each case it was selected to make the local hour angle come out to a whole degree, but in one instance you have calculated the local hour angle of Aries, and in the other, the local hour angle of the star itself. As you will see if you plot the position lines, the two lines will be virtually coincident, as long as you remember to plot each one from its respective assumed position.

In the Volume II/III method, after calculating the local hour angle of the star, and having already found the star's declination in the almanac list, and assumed a latitude (41°) near your DR position, you are ready to enter the sight reduction tables in the regular way. The excerpt in Figure 9–6 shows the data we seek. At Latitude 41°, with the declination of the same name, North, descend the LHA column to 341°, the value we had found for Arcturus's

---

Figure 9–6. **Excerpt from Volume III, Pub. No. 249, showing that at Latitude 41°, same name as declination, at LHA 341°, and declination 19°, Hc is 62°40′, *d* is +50′, and Z, 138°**

N. Lat. { LHA greater than 180°.......Zn=Z
LHA less than 180°..........Zn=360−Z

LAT 41° DECLINATION (15°-29°) SAME NAME AS LATITUDE

LHA	15° Hc	15° d	15° Z	16° Hc	16° d	16° Z	17° Hc	17° d	17° Z	18° Hc	18° d	18° Z	19° Hc	19° d	19° Z
	° ′	′	°	° ′	′	°	° ′	′	°	° ′	′	°	° ′	′	°
0	64 00	+60	180	65 00	+60	180	66 00	+60	180	67 00	+60	180	68 00	+60	180
1	63 59	60	178	64 59	60	178	65 59	60	178	66 59	60	178	67 59	60	178
2	63 57	59	176	64 56	60	176	65 56	60	175	66 56	60	175	67 56	60	175
3	63 52	60	173	64 52	60	173	65 52	59	173	66 51	60	173	67 51	60	173
4	63 46	60	171	64 46	59	171	65 45	60	171	66 45	59	170	67 44	60	170
5	63 38	+60	169	64 38	+59	169	65 37	+59	168	66 36	+59	168	67 35	+59	168
6	63 29	59	167	64 28	59	167	65 27	59	166	66 26	59	166	67 25	58	165
7	63 18	59	165	64 17	58	164	65 15	59	164	66 14	58	163	67 12	58	163
8	63 05	59	163	64 04	58	162	65 02	58	162	66 00	59	161	66 58	57	160
9	62 51	58	161	63 49	58	160	64 47	57	159	65 44	58	159	66 42	57	158
10	62 35	+58	159	63 33	+57	158	64 30	+57	157	65 27	+57	157	66 24	+56	156
11	62 18	57	157	63 15	57	156	64 12	56	155	65 08	57	154	66 05	55	154
12	61 59	57	155	62 56	56	154	63 52	56	153	64 48	56	152	65 44	55	151
13	61 39	56	153	62 35	56	152	63 31	55	151	64 26	55	150	65 21	55	149
14	61 18	55	151	62 13	55	150	63 08	55	149	64 03	54	148	64 57	54	147
15	60 55	+55	149	61 50	+55	148	62 45	+54	147	63 39	+53	146	64 32	+54	145
16	60 31	55	147	61 26	53	146	62 19	54	145	63 13	53	144	64 06	52	143
17	60 06	54	146	61 00	53	145	61 53	53	144	62 46	52	143	63 38	52	142
18	59 40	53	144	60 33	53	143	61 26	52	142	62 18	52	141	63 10	51	140
19	59 13	52	142	60 05	52	141	60 57	52	140	61 49	51	139	62 40	50	138
20	58 45	+51	141	59 36	+52	140	60 28	+51	138	61 19	+50	137	62 09	+50	136
21	58 15	51	139	59 06	51	138	59 57	50	137	60 47	50	136	61 37	49	135
22	57 45	51	137	58 36	50	136	59 26	49	135	60 15	49	134	61 04	49	133
23	57 14	50	136	58 04	49	135	58 53	49	134	59 42	49	133	60 31	47	131
24	56 42	49	134	57 31	49	133	58 20	49	132	59 09	47	131	59 56	47	130

20° Hc	20° d	20° Z	21° Hc	21° d	21° Z	22° Hc	22° d	22° Z	23° Hc	23° d	23° Z	24° Hc	24° d	24° Z	LHA
° ′	′	°	° ′	′	°	° ′	′	°	° ′	′	°	° ′	′	°	
69 00	+60	180	70 00	+60	180	71 00	+60	180	72 00	+60	180	73 00	+60	180	360
68 59	60	177	69 59	60	177	70 59	60	177	71 59	60	177	72 59	60	177	359
68 56	60	175	69 56	60	175	70 56	59	174	71 55	60	174	72 55	60	174	358
68 51	59	172	69 50	60	172	70 50	60	172	71 50	59	171	72 49	59	171	357
68 44	59	170	69 43	59	169	70 42	59	169	71 41	59	168	72 40	59	168	356
68 34	+59	167	69 33	+59	167	70 32	+59	166	71 31	+59	165	72 30	+58	165	355
68 23	59	165	69 22	58	164	70 20	58	163	71 18	59	163	72 17	57	162	354
68 10	58	162	69 08	58	161	70 06	58	161	71 04	57	160	72 01	57	159	353
67 55	58	160	68 53	57	159	69 50	57	158	70 47	57	157	71 44	56	156	352
67 39	57	157	68 36	56	156	69 32	57	156	70 29	56	155	71 25	55	153	351
67 20	+57	155	68 17	+56	154	69 13	+55	153	70 08	+55	152	71 03	+55	151	350
67 00	56	153	67 56	55	152	68 51	55	151	69 46	54	150	70 40	54	148	349
66 39	55	151	67 34	54	149	68 28	54	148	69 22	54	147	70 16	52	146	348
66 16	54	148	67 10	54	147	68 04	53	146	68 57	52	145	69 49	52	143	347
65 51	54	146	66 45	53	145	67 38	52	144	68 30	52	143	69 22	51	141	346
65 26	+52	144	66 18	+52	143	67 10	+52	142	68 02	+51	140	68 53	+50	139	345
64 58	52	142	65 50	52	141	66 42	50	140	67 32	50	138	68 22	49	137	344
64 30	51	140	65 21	51	139	66 12	50	138	67 02	49	136	67 51	48	135	343
64 01	50	139	64 51	50	137	65 41	49	136	66 30	48	135	67 18	48	133	342
63 30	50	137	64 20	49	135	65 09	48	134	65 57	48	133	66 45	46	131	341
62 59	+49	135	63 48	+48	134	64 36	+47	132	65 23	+47	131	66 10	+46	129	340
62 26	48	133	63 14	48	132	64 02	47	131	64 49	46	129	65 35	44	128	339
61 53	47	132	62 40	47	130	63 27	46	129	64 13	45	128	64 58	44	126	338
61 18	47	130	62 05	47	129	62 52	45	127	63 37	44	126	64 21	44	124	337
60 43	47	129	61 30	45	127	62 15	45	126	63 00	44	124	63 44	42	123	336

local hour angle. Opposite the LHA, in the column containing the whole degrees, 19°, of Arcturus's declination (19°15.9′N), you fnd the tabular Hc, 62°40′, and the azimuth angle, Z, 138°. The altitude differential, *d*, you will note, is +50′. Turning to Table 5, Figure 9–7, the correction to the tabulated altitude for 15.9′ of declination at a *d*-value of +50, is 13′. This correction, added to the tabular value produces a computed altitude of 62°53′, which when compared with the observed altitude, yields an intercept of 4.4′ "toward." Since the LHA of 341° is greater than 180°, the rule in this case is that Zn equals Z,

43	44	45	46	47	48	49	50	51	52	53	54	55	56	57	58	59	60	*d* ′
0	0	0	0	0	0	0	0	0	0	0	0	0	0	0	0	0	0	0
1	1	1	1	1	1	1	1	1	1	1	1	1	1	1	1	1	1	1
1	1	2	2	2	2	2	2	2	2	2	2	2	2	2	2	2	2	2
2	2	2	2	2	2	2	2	3	3	3	3	3	3	3	3	3	3	3
3	3	3	3	3	3	3	3	3	3	4	4	4	4	4	4	4	4	4
4	4	4	4	4	4	4	4	4	4	4	4	5	5	5	5	5	5	5
4	4	4	5	5	5	5	5	5	5	5	5	6	6	6	6	6	6	6
5	5	5	5	5	6	6	6	6	6	6	6	6	7	7	7	7	7	7
6	6	6	6	6	6	7	7	7	7	7	7	7	7	8	8	8	8	8
6	7	7	7	7	7	7	8	8	8	8	8	8	8	9	9	9	9	9
7	7	8	8	8	8	8	8	8	9	9	9	9	9	10	10	10	10	10
8	8	8	8	9	9	9	9	9	10	10	10	10	10	10	11	11	11	11
9	9	9	9	9	10	10	10	10	10	11	11	11	11	11	12	12	12	12
9	10	10	10	10	10	11	11	11	11	11	12	12	12	12	13	13	13	13
10	10	10	11	11	11	11	12	12	12	12	13	13	13	13	14	14	14	14
11	11	11	12	12	12	12	12	13	13	13	14	14	14	14	14	15	15	15
11	12	12	12	13	13	13	13	14	14	14	14	15	15	15	15	16	16	16
12	12	13	13	13	14	14	14	14	15	15	15	16	16	16	16	17	17	17
13	13	14	14	14	14	15	15	15	16	16	16	16	17	17	17	18	18	18
14	14	14	15	15	15	16	16	16	16	17	17	17	18	18	18	19	19	19
14	15	15	15	16	16	16	17	17	17	18	18	18	19	19	19	20	20	20
15	15	16	16	16	17	17	18	18	18	19	19	19	20	20	20	21	21	21
16	16	16	17	17	18	18	18	19	19	19	20	20	21	21	21	22	22	22
16	17	17	18	18	18	19	19	20	20	20	21	21	21	22	22	23	23	23
17	18	18	18	19	19	20	20	20	21	21	22	22	22	23	23	24	24	24

Figure 9–7. **Excerpt from Table 5, Pub. No. 249, showing a correction of 13′ for *d* of 50, and incremental minutes of declination, 16**

and the true azimuth is 138°. Except for the rounding off which is inherent in the process and may create minor differences, Arcturus's line of position, properly plotted, will be the same line as the one derived in the Volume I solution, as has been explained.

By now, you will have correctly concluded that reducing star sights is no more difficult than reducing any other observation—with Volume I, perhaps, stars are even easier—so why all the concern expressed earlier? The problem lies in the process of taking, timing, and recording star sights, and when you first try to do it by yourself, you will understand the challenge in getting precise results.

First, of course, you have to identify the star you are shooting. Unlike the familiar bodies in the solar system, a star's identification is not obvious, especially during twilight when the constellations, by which most observers relate a star's position in the sky, may not be totally visible. Unless you have been observing the same body night after night, the most practical solution is preplanning. To do this, you need to estimate the approximate time you expect to be taking your sights, and that can be done either by knowing the time of twilight by previous observation, or by calculating it from the auxiliary tables in the almanac's daily pages (Figure 3–2). With the estimated time of observation converted to Greenwich mean time, you can find the Greenwich hour angle of Aries, just as you do in working a star sight, and by applying an estimate of your expected longitude at twilight, you can calculate the approximate local hour angle of Aries. Then, you can follow one of two recommended routes: You can enter Volume I of Pub. No. 249 (Figure 9–4), and opposite the approximate LHA♈, read out the seven selected stars and their altitudes and azimuths; or you can use a device called a star-finder.

The first way is the simplest and quickest, and is particularly to be recommended if you intend to work your sights with Volume I. If you prefer to predict the positions of all the visible stars, to give yourself the widest possible choice, the best device, in my opinion, is the Rude Star Finder. Originally developed for the Navy, and now offered commercially, the star-finder consists of a base and a series of transparent templates for each 10° of latitude. The appropriate template is placed over the circular base and oriented to the estimated local hour angle of Aries. The altitudes and azimuths of all the visible navigational stars can then be found by inspection. However you choose to do your star-finding, adopt the technique of the most experienced navigators, and prepare ahead of time a list of the approximate altitudes and azimuths of the stars you expect to shoot. It will simplify matters considerably when you go on deck.

The idea behind star observations is no more complicated than for any other sight. You measure the altitude by centering the reflected image on the horizon, immediately record it along with the exact time, and then move on to the next star. On small boats, and especially in a seaway, the problem is that you have to perform all the operations and hold on at the same time; with only two hands, it is not so easy. The problem is magnified by the narrow span between the time the sky is too bright to see the stars, and the time it is too dark to see the horizon; and the low level of luminosity, which makes a star's image indistinct, doesn't help. The finer optics and larger field of view of the better sextants alleviate the problem somewhat, but star sights are seldom as easy as those of the sun.

You can usually find a star in the sextant's field of view by presetting the estimated altitude from your prepared list, and panning along the horizon at the star's approximate azimuth. Alternatively, you can hold the sextant upside down with your left hand, aim it directly at the star, and having located the star through the eyepiece, move the index arm with your right hand to bring the horizon up to the star. This done, reverse the sextant, and the star's image should be close to the visible horizon. This latter technique is easiest with a straight telescope for an eyepiece, but if you prefer to use a monocular like the one illustrated in Figure 1–1, it will require some practice.

Should you be fortunate enough to have a shipmate available to help you, the task of taking star sights will be immeasurably easier. He can read off the estimated altitudes and azimuths from your prepared list, and can take and record the exact time of each observation as you call out, "Mark." Your night vision won't be affected by having to use a light, you can concentrate fully on the sextant manipulation, and you will have the best opportunity to complete a round of good sights within the narrow twilight period. Even under these happy circumstances, however, I reiterate my comment made at the onset: Under the normal conditions aboard a small boat at sea, the sun is a more constant companion to a conscientious navigator.

10 Special Cases

Although the majority of celestial observations are converted to lines of position by means of the techniques described in the preceding chapters, you can also take advantage of two special situations: shortcut solutions for finding the latitude by observation of the sun at local apparent noon (LAN), or by observation of Polaris, the pole star.

The most common of these special cases is the noon sight of the sun. Technically called "latitude by meridian altitude," the process of obtaining a quick and reliable latitude check by means of a single reduction of a sun sight at the moment the sun's path crosses the meridian of the observer and reaches its highest point of the day is a mariner's tradition. No one knows with certainty when the technique was first practiced, but the concept was well understood by the time the astrolabe appeared in the third century B.C., and as increasingly accurate altitude-measuring instruments evolved, the use of noon latitudes became universal. By the fifteenth century, it was common practice on long passages to run down to the latitude of a destination, to a point well to seaward of it, and then to shape the course east or west until a landfall was made, using noon sights all the way. Even today, the noon observation is a ritual, performed as it has been for years, aboard Navy and merchant ships.

For a navigator, the special appeal of a noon sight is that the sun's altitude is changing very slowly at the time, thereby reducing the need for precise time measurement. Then, too, after an observation has been made, the calculation needed to determine the latitude is simple and rapid—whether done manually or with a calculator—and the only piece of astronomical information required is the sun's declination. While, for the reasons given, the *exact* time of local apparent noon is not essential, as it is in normal sights, it is useful to predict the approximate time when LAN will occur, so that the navigator can come on deck a few minutes early for an unhurried series of observations. There are a number of ways to predict the time of local apparent noon, three of which are commonly used by yacht navigators.

The first way, called the "GHA method," is based on the fact that at the moment of meridian passage, the local hour angle of the sun is zero. Remembering the formula,

$$\text{LHA} = \text{GHA} \genfrac{}{}{0pt}{}{-\text{West}}{+\text{East}} \text{Longitude}$$

the Greenwich hour angle of the sun at LAN must be the same as your longitude if West, or 360° minus the longitude if East. Accordingly, the procedure is first to estimate what you expect your longitude to be about the time of local apparent noon—this can be done simply by running your position ahead by dead reckoning—and then, entering the SUN column of the almanac's correct daily page, find the GHA *next smaller* than your longitude, and note the hours of Greenwich mean time opposite that GHA. Next, subtract the selected GHA from the longitude, and use that difference to enter the *Increments and Corrections* tables in reverse—that is, you enter the body of the table to locate the increment in the SUN column equal to the difference you just calculated, and read out the minutes and seconds of time that correspond to that increment. The hours you noted on the daily page, and the minutes and seconds of time from the increment table, represent the time of LAN expressed as Greenwich mean time. It is a simple matter to convert that to local watch time by applying the zone description.

Let's look at a practical example. On June 8, 1984, a navigator estimates that his longitude about the time of LAN will be 70°07.5′W. Entering the SUN column of the *Nautical Almanac* with this estimated longitude (Figure 10–1), he finds that the next smaller GHA is 60°14.0′ at 16 hours GMT. Subtracting the tabular GHA from the longi-

1984 JUNE 8

G.M.T.		SUN G.H.A.		Dec.	
d	h	°	′	°	′
8	00	180	15.9	N22	50.6
	01	195	15.8		50.9
	02	210	15.7		51.1
	03	225	15.5	··	51.3
	04	240	15.4		51.5
	05	255	15.3		51.8
	06	270	15.2	N22	52.0
	07	285	15.1		52 2
	08	300	14.9		52.4
F	09	315	14.8	··	52.6
R	10	330	14.7		52.9
I	11	345	14.6		53.1
D	12	0	14.5	N22	53.3
A	13	15	14.3		53.5
Y	14	30	14.2		53.7
	15	45	14.1	··	54.0
	16	60	14.0		54.2
	17	75	13.9		54.4
	18	90	13.7	N22	54.6
	19	105	13.6		54.8
	20	120	13.5		55.0
	21	135	13.4	··	55.2
	22	150	13.3		55.4
	23	165	13.1		55.7

Figure 10–1. **Excerpt from the *Nautical Almanac* for June 8, 1984, showing GHA of 60°14′ opposite GMT 16 hours. At 1639 GMT, the declination is found to be 22°54.3′N.**

tude produces a difference of 9°53.5′, and turning to the *Increments and Corrections* tables in the back of the almanac, Figure 10–2, he finds the equivalent increment in the SUN column for 39 minutes and 34 seconds of time. The estimated time of LAN, therefore, is 16:39:34, or if the ship is keeping Eastern Daylight Saving Time (ZD +4), the local time would read 12:39:34.

A second, even quicker solution can be found by the "meridian passage method." If you are good at mental arithmetic, and can accept a little more of an approximation, the local time of LAN can be determined virtually by inspection. In this method, you take the time of the sun's meridian passage from the box on the lower right-hand side of the almanac's daily page (Figure 10–3), and adjust it by the difference, expressed in time, between the

INCREMENTS AND CORRECTIONS 39m

39m	SUN PLANETS	ARIES	MOON	v or d	Corrn	v or d	Corrn	v or d	Corrn
s	° ′	° ′	° ′	′	′	′	′	′	′
00	9 45·0	9 46·6	9 18·4	0·0	0·0	6·0	4·0	12·0	7·9
01	9 45·3	9 46·9	9 18·6	0·1	0·1	6·1	4·0	12·1	8·0
02	9 45·5	9 47·1	9 18·8	0·2	0·1	6·2	4·1	12·2	8·0
03	9 45·8	9 47·4	9 19·1	0·3	0·2	6·3	4·1	12·3	8·1
28	[illegible]	[illegible]	[illegible]	[illegible]	[illegible]	[illegible]	[illegible]	[illegible]	[illegible]
29	9 52·3	9 53·9	9 25·3	2·9	1·9	8·9	5·9	14·9	9·8
30	9 52·5	9 54·1	9 25·5	3·0	2·0	9·0	5·9	15·0	9·9
31	9 52·8	9 54·4	9 25·7	3·1	2·0	9·1	6·0	15·1	9·9
32	9 53·0	9 54·6	9 26·0	3·2	2·1	9·2	6·1	15·2	10·0
33	9 53·3	9 54·9	9 26·2	3·3	2·2	9·3	6·1	15·3	10·1
34	9 53·5	9 55·1	9 26·5	3·4	2·2	9·4	6·2	15·4	10·1
35	9 53·8	9 55·4	9 26·7	3·5	2·3	9·5	6·3	15·5	10·2
36	9 54·0	9 55·6	9 26·9	3·6	2·4	9·6	6·3	15·6	10·3
37	9 54·3	9 55·9	9 27·2	3·7	2·4	9·7	6·4	15·7	10·3
38	9 54·5	9 56·1	9 27·4	3·8	2·5	9·8	6·5	15·8	10·4
39	9 54·8	9 56·4	9 27·7	3·9	2·6	9·9	6·5	15·9	10·5

Figure 10–2. **Excerpt from the *Nautical Almanac* increments and corrections tables showing the increment 9°53.5′ corresponding to 39 minutes, 34 seconds of time**

Day	SUN Eqn. of Time 00ʰ	12ʰ	Mer. Pass.
	m s	m s	h m
8	01 04	00 58	11 59
9	00 52	00 46	11 59
10	00 41	00 35	11 59

Figure 10–3. **Excerpt from the *Nautical Almanac* daily page June 8, 1984, showing sun's meridian passage to occur at 1159, and Equation of Time at 12ʰ to be 00 minutes, 58 seconds**

estimated noon longitude and the nearest standard, or zone meridian. In our practical example, the difference between the estimated longitude, 70°07.5′W, and the nearest standard meridian, 75°W, is 4°52.5′. Since the sun moves 15° per hour, or 1° every 4′, 4°52.5′ represents an adjustment of just under 20′ in time, and because the estimated longitude is east of the standard meridian, the correction must be subtracted from the tabular time of meridian passage, 1159, to produce the local time of LAN, 1139. The adjustment can be made more precise by taking the exact longitude difference, 4°52.5′, and by means of the arc-to-time conversion table in the back of the almanac (Figure 10–4), find the exact time correction, 19 minutes, 30 seconds. This would mean a local time of LAN of 11:39:30, or 12:39:30 if daylight time is being kept.

A third method for finding the time of local apparent noon, the "equation-of-time method," is based on the Equation of Time, which is the difference between the time of the fictitious, mean sun and the apparent solar, or "sundial" time. The equation of time for 12 hours, as seen

Figure 10–4. **Table from *Nautical Almanac* for converting arc to time. 4°52.5′ is the equivalent of 19 minutes, 30 seconds of time.**

CONVERSION OF ARC TO TIME

–59°	60°–119°		120°–179°		180°–239°		240°–299°		300°–359°			0'.00	0'.25	0'.50	0'.75
h m	°	h m	°	h m	°	h m	°	h m	°	h m	'	m s	m s	m s	m s
0 00	60	4 00	120	8 00	180	12 00	240	16 00	300	20 00	0	0 00	0 01	0 02	0 03
0 04	61	4 04	121	8 04	181	12 04	241	16 04	301	20 04	1	0 04	0 05	0 06	0 07
0 08	62	4 08	122	8 08	182	12 08	242	16 08	302	20 08	2	0 08	0 09	0 10	0 11
0 12	63	4 12	123	8 12	183	12 12	243	16 12	303	20 12	3	0 12	0 13	0 14	0 15
0 16	64	4 16	124	8 16	184	12 16	244	16 16	304	20 16	4	0 16	0 17	0 18	0 19
0 20	65	4 20	125	8 20	185	12 20	245	16 20	305	20 20	5	0 20	0 21	0 22	0 23
0 24	66	4 24	126	8 24	186	12 24	246	16 24	306	20 24	6	0 24	0 25	0 26	0 27
0 28	67	4 28	127	8 28	187	12 28	247	16 28	307	20 28	7	0 28	0 29	0 30	0 31
0 32	68	4 32	128	8 32	188	12 32	248	16 32	308	20 32	8	0 32	0 33	0 34	0 35
0 36	69	4 36	129	8 36	189	12 36	249	16 36	309	20 36	9	0 36	0 37	0 38	0 39
0 40	70	4 40	130	8 40	190	12 40	250	16 40	310	20 40	10	0 40	0 41	0 42	0 43
0 44	71	4 44	131	8 44	191	12 44	251	16 44	311	20 44	11	0 44	0 45	0 46	0 47
0 48	72	4 48	132	8 48	192	12 48	252	16 48	312	20 48	12	0 48	0 49	0 50	0 51
0 52	73	4 52	133	8 52	193	12 52	253	16 52	313	20 52	13	0 52	0 53	0 54	0 55
0 56	74	4 56	134	8 56	194	12 56	254	16 56	314	20 56	14	0 56	0 57	0 58	0 59
1 00	75	5 00	135	9 00	195	13 00	255	17 00	315	21 00	15	1 00	1 01	1 02	1 03
1 04	76	5 04	136	9 04	196	13 04	256	17 04	316	21 04	16	1 04	1 05	1 06	1 07
1 08	77	5 08	137	9 08	197	13 08	257	17 08	317	21 08	17	1 08	1 09	1 10	1 11
1 12	78	5 12	138	9 12	198	13 12	258	17 12	318	21 12	18	1 12	1 13	1 14	1 15
1 16	79	5 16	139	9 16	199	13 16	259	17 16	319	21 16	19	1 16	1 17	1 18	1 19
1 20	80	5 20	140	9 20	200	13 20	260	17 20	320	21 20	20	1 20	1 21	1 22	1 23
1 24	81	5 24	141	9 24	201	13 24	261	17 24	321	21 24	21	1 24	1 25	1 26	1 27
1 28	82	5 28	142	9 28	202	13 28	262	17 28	322	21 28	22	1 28	1 29	1 30	1 31
1 32	83	5 32	143	9 32	203	13 32	263	17 32	323	21 32	23	1 32	1 33	1 34	1 35
1 36	84	5 36	144	9 36	204	13 36	264	17 36	324	21 36	24	1 36	1 37	1 38	1 39
1 40	85	5 40	145	9 40	205	13 40	265	17 40	325	21 40	25	1 40	1 41	1 42	1 43
1 44	86	5 44	146	9 44	206	13 44	266	17 44	326	21 44	26	1 44	1 45	1 46	1 47
1 48	87	5 48	147	9 48	207	13 48	267	17 48	327	21 48	27	1 48	1 49	1 50	1 51
1 52	88	5 52	148	9 52	208	13 52	268	17 52	328	21 52	28	1 52	1 53	1 54	1 55
1 56	89	5 56	149	9 56	209	13 56	269	17 56	329	21 56	29	1 56	1 57	1 58	1 59
2 00	90	6 00	150	10 00	210	14 00	270	18 00	330	22 00	30	2 00	2 01	2 02	2 03
2 04	91	6 04	151	10 04	211	14 04	271	18 04	331	22 04	31	2 04	2 05	2 06	2 07
2 08	92	6 08	152	10 08	212	14 08	272	18 08	332	22 08	32	2 08	2 09	2 10	2 11
2 12	93	6 12	153	10 12	213	14 12	273	18 12	333	22 12	33	2 12	2 13	2 14	2 15
2 16	94	6 16	154	10 16	214	14 16	274	18 16	334	22 16	34	2 16	2 17	2 18	2 19
2 20	95	6 20	155	10 20	215	14 20	275	18 20	335	22 20	35	2 20	2 21	2 22	2 23
2 24	96	6 24	156	10 24	216	14 24	276	18 24	336	22 24	36	2 24	2 25	2 26	2 27
2 28	97	6 28	157	10 28	217	14 28	277	18 28	337	22 28	37	2 28	2 29	2 30	2 31
2 32	98	6 32	158	10 32	218	14 32	278	18 32	338	22 32	38	2 32	2 33	2 34	2 35
2 36	99	6 36	159	10 36	219	14 36	279	18 36	339	22 36	39	2 36	2 37	2 38	2 39
2 40	100	6 40	160	10 40	220	14 40	280	18 40	340	22 40	40	2 40	2 41	2 42	2 43
2 44	101	6 44	161	10 44	221	14 44	281	18 44	341	22 44	41	2 44	2 45	2 46	2 47
2 48	102	6 48	162	10 48	222	14 48	282	18 48	342	22 48	42	2 48	2 49	2 50	2 51
2 52	103	6 52	163	10 52	223	14 52	283	18 52	343	22 52	43	2 52	2 53	2 54	2 55
2 56	104	6 56	164	10 56	224	14 56	284	18 56	344	22 56	44	2 56	2 57	2 58	2 59
3 00	105	7 00	165	11 00	225	15 00	285	19 00	345	23 00	45	3 00	3 01	3 02	3 03
3 04	106	7 04	166	11 04	226	15 04	286	19 04	346	23 04	46	3 04	3 05	3 06	3 07
3 08	107	7 08	167	11 08	227	15 08	287	19 08	347	23 08	47	3 08	3 09	3 10	3 11
3 12	108	7 12	168	11 12	228	15 12	288	19 12	348	23 12	48	3 12	3 13	3 14	3 15
3 16	109	7 16	169	11 16	229	15 16	289	19 16	349	23 16	49	3 16	3 17	3 18	3 19
3 20	110	7 20	170	11 20	230	15 20	290	19 20	350	23 20	50	3 20	3 21	3 22	3 23
3 24	111	7 24	171	11 24	231	15 24	291	19 24	351	23 24	51	3 24	3 25	3 26	3 27
3 28	112	7 28	172	11 28	232	15 28	292	19 28	352	23 28	52	3 28	3 29	3 30	3 31
3 32	113	7 32	173	11 32	233	15 32	293	19 32	353	23 32	53	3 32	3 33	3 34	3 35
3 36	114	7 36	174	11 36	234	15 36	294	19 36	354	23 36	54	3 36	3 37	3 38	3 39
3 40	115	7 40	175	11 40	235	15 40	295	19 40	355	23 40	55	3 40	3 41	3 42	3 43
3 44	116	7 44	176	11 44	236	15 44	296	19 44	356	23 44	56	3 44	3 45	3 46	3 47
3 48	117	7 48	177	11 48	237	15 48	297	19 48	357	23 48	57	3 48	3 49	3 50	3 51
3 52	118	7 52	178	11 52	238	15 52	298	19 52	358	23 52	58	3 52	3 53	3 54	3 55
3 56	119	7 56	179	11 56	239	15 56	299	19 56	359	23 56	59	3 56	3 57	3 58	3 59

The above table is for converting expressions in arc to their equivalent in time ; its main use in this Almanac
the conversion of longitude for application to L.M.T. (*added* if *west*, *subtracted* if *east*) to give G.M.T. or vice
particularly in the case of sunrise, sunset, etc.

in Figure 10–3, is 00 minutes, 58 seconds on June 8, and the formula is:

GMT of LAN = Estimated longitude ÷ 15 + 12 ± Equation of time

The equation of time is subtracted if the listed meridian passage occurs before 1200, as in our case, or it is added if the meridian passage takes place after noon. Applying the formula to our practical example, the Greenwich mean time of LAN works out to be 16:39:32.

In any of the methods described, the accuracy of the predicted time of LAN is only as good as your estimate of the longitude. As a consequence, if the time you calculate for LAN turns out to be quite different from the time you used for estimating the longitude originally, it is a good idea to reestimate the longitude at a time closer to your calculated LAN, and then run through the procedure a second time.

The technique in making the actual noon observation of the sun consists of measuring the sun's altitude (usually the lower limb) at the highest point of its arc. In practice, the navigator begins shooting several minutes before the predicted time of LAN and, through a series of observations, follows the sun's altitude up until it appears to "hang" at the highest point before starting to descend. Some navigators plot each successive altitude on a graph in order to be certain of the highest reading, but I have never found this to be necessary. On the other hand, if the sky is at all obscured, it is a good idea to record the time and altitude of one or more of your good sights, so that if you miss the noon shot, you can still work out the sight by the regular method. Most of the time, however, a simple series of observations is all that is needed, recording only the maximum altitude, and then calculating the latitude directly by the following steps:

- The sextant altitude is corrected in exactly the same way as any normal sun sight, obtaining the observed altitude, Ho, which is marked with the sun's bearing from you, North or South.

- The observed altitude is subtracted from 90°, arriving at an intermediate value, zenith distance, z, which is marked with the name *opposite* to the sun's bearing.
- The sun's declination for the estimated time of LAN (expressed as Greenwich mean time) is taken from the almanac and added to z if of the same name, or the difference is taken if the names are opposite. The result is the observer's latitude, with the name of the larger of z or declination.

Let's return to our practical example, and assume that at local apparent noon on June 8, 1984, the sun's maximum altitude measures 71°58.0′, its bearing is South, the sextant's index correction is –2.4′, and the dip correction is –2.9′ for a height of eye of 9 feet. The completed workform, with which you can follow the noon-sight solution, looks like this:

DATE	June 8, 1984
Est. λ	70-07.5 W
Std. Mer.	75 W
Corr in time	-19-30
Mer. Pass.	11-59-00
LAN	11-39-30
GMT	16-39-30
hs	71-58.0
IC	-2.4
D	-2.9
ha	71-52.7
R	+15.6
Ho	72-08.3 S
90°	89-60.0
−Ho	72-08.3 S
z	17-51.7 N
Dec	22-54.3 N
L	40-46.0 °
(name)	N

Starting with the estimated longitude of 70°07.5′W, the meridian passage method is used to predict the time of LAN. The almanac's arc-to-time table, Figure 10–4, shows the difference in time, corresponding to the 4° 52.5′-difference in longitude between the estimated longitude and the standard meridian, to be 19 minutes, 30 seconds. Because the observer's longitude is east of the standard meridian, the time difference is subtracted from the 1159 time of meridian passage listed in the almanac (Figure 10–3), producing a Greenwich mean time of LAN at 16:39:30. The sextant altitude is corrected for index error and dip in the usual way, arriving at an apparent altitude, ha, of 71°52.7′, and the apparent altitude is further adjusted for the refraction, or R-correction, of +15.6′ found in the regular sun-altitude correction table (Figure 10–5). The resulting observed altitude, Ho, of 72°08.3′ is marked South (from the sun's bearing), and is subtracted from 90° to obtain the zenith distance, z, of 17° 51.7′, which is marked North, the name opposite the sun's bearing. In the SUN column of the almanac's daily page, Figure 10–1, the sun's declination for the predicted time of LAN is found to be 22°54.3′N. Since declination and z are of the same name, the rule calls for them to be added, yielding the latitude, 40°46.0′, which is North, the name of the declination, which is larger than z.

As you can see, this is a very easy way to produce a good latitude line, and it works well in all circumstances, with the possible exception of a vessel on a northerly or southerly course traveling at high speed. In that situation the sun's measured altitude may still appear to be changing at the predicted time of meridian passage, and to avoid error, it is better to measure one good altitude, time it precisely, and work the sight for a regular line of position.

Since, as we have discussed, the sun's Greenwich hour angle is equal to your West longitude (or 360° minus

A2 ALTITUDE CORRECTION TABLES 10°-90°

OCT.—MAR.	SUN		APR.—SEPT.			DIP				
App. Alt.	Lower Limb	Upper Limb	App. Alt.	Lower Limb	Upper Limb	Ht. of Eye	Corrⁿ	Ht. of Eye	Ht. of Eye	Corrⁿ
						m		ft.	m	
50 40			52 44			2·4		8·0	1·0	1·8
	+15·5	−16·8		+15·3	−16·5		−2·8		1·5	2·2
54 49			57 02			2·6		8·6	2·0	2·5
	+15·6	−16·7		+15·4	−16·4		−2·9		2·5	2·8
59 23			61 51			2·8		9·2	3·0	3·0
	+15·7	−16·6		+15·5	−16·3		−3·0		See table ←	
64 30			67 17			3·0		9·8		
	+15·8	16·5		+15·6	−16·2		−3·1			
70 12			73 16			3·2		10·5		
	+15·9	−16·4		+15·7	−16·1		−3·2			
76 26			79 43			3·4		11·2		
	+16·0	−16·3		+15·8	−16·0		−3·3			
83 05			86 32			3·6		11·9		
	+16·1	16·2		+15·9	−15·9					
90 00			90 00							

Figure 10–5. **Excerpt from the *Nautical Almanac*'s altitude correction tables showing a dip correction of –2.9′ for a height of eye of 9 feet, and an R-correction of +15.6′ for the apparent altitude, 71°52.7′**

East longitude) at local apparent noon, it should be possible in theory, given the *exact* time of LAN, to look up the sun's Greenwich hour angle for that moment, and to use that GHA to make a direct determination of your longitude. The difficulty, however, lies in obtaining a sufficiently precise timing of the instant that the sun attains its maximum altitude, because, as you will observe, the altitude changes almost imperceptibly for a short time before or after its peak. Some navigators try by beginning their series of observations 15 minutes or more prior to the predicted time of LAN, recording or plotting the time and altitude of each sight as the sun ascends, and then, as the readings start to decrease, taking the time of each matching altitude. In concept, the actual time of LAN can then be calculated by averaging the times of common altitudes, but the procedure requires a lot of time and effort. Should clouds or sea conditions, or the vessel's own movement during the series, introduce an error into some of the sights, the results are apt to be inconclusive. With accurate time available, it is usually better to use the LAN observation just for latitude, and to rely on regular sun lines at other times during the day.

A second special case allowing the direct determination of latitude is an observation of Polaris, the pole star, at morning or evening twilight. Although you may not use the technique as often as the noon sight, a Polaris observation works anywhere in the Northern Hemisphere, and shares with the noon sun the distinction of being one of the earliest exercises in nautical astronomy—possibly because the star is so easy to identify. Despite the fact that Polaris is a second magnitude star (Mag. 2.1, to be exact), anyone at all familiar with the night sky knows how to find it by following the pointers from the Big Dipper. More sophisticated observers can also spot Polaris's position in relation to the constellation Cassiopeia, the flattened "W" opposite the Dipper. The special quality of Polaris, which makes the solution for latitude so easy, is its constant position within a degree or so of the North Celestial Pole. Since the altitude of the celestial pole is equivalent to the observer's latitude, it is only a question of correcting the sextant altitude, and adjusting for the exact position of the star, to obtain a precise latitude. The steps are simple and straightforward.

- Correct the sextant altitude, hs, in the same manner as for any star sight, to obtain the observed altitude, Ho.
- Calculate LHA of Aries by applying your estimated longitude to GHA Aries found in the almanac for the time of observation.
- Enter the Polaris tables (at the back of the *Nautical Almanac*, and extract the value of a_0, for the corresponding LHA♈; a_1, for the estimated latitude; and a_2, for the month of observation.

• Then, Ho $-1° + a_0 + a_1 + a_2 =$ latitude, and since Polaris is visible only in the Northern Hemisphere, the latitude is always North.

Let's review the Polaris procedure with a practical example. Returning from the Bahamas on March 16, 1984, a navigator estimates his position at evening twilight to be at Latitude 26°41.2′N, Longitude 79°31.9′W. At 18:51:09 local time (23:51:09 GMT), he observes Polaris on the starboard beam at an altitude of 27°16.8′. The sextant's index correction is –2.4′, and the observer's height of eye is 9 feet. What is his precise latitude? As with our other sights, we will use a workform to follow the solution step by step.

DATE	March 16, 1984
hs	27-16.8
IC	-2.4
D	-2.9
ha	27-11.5
R	-1.9
Ho	27-09.6
W	23-51-09
corr	00
GMT	23-51-09
gha ♈	159-42.5
incr	12-49.4
GHA ♈	172-31.9
a λ	79-31.9
LHA ♈	93-00
a L	26-41 N
Ho	27-09.6
−1°	26-09.6
$+a_0$	34.3
$+a_1$	0.4
$+a_2$	0.9
L	26-45.2 N

In the regular way, applicable to all observations, the IC and D-corrections adjust our sextant altitude of 27° 16.8′ to an apparent altitude of 27°11.5′, and the R-correction, found in the STARS column of the almanac tables to be –1.9′ (Figure 10–6), then produces an observed altitude of 27°09.6′. Polaris's position is presented in the almanac as a function of the local hour angle of Aries, so we must next determine LHA ♈, again following the procedure for any normal star sight. The Greenwich hour angle of Aries is found in the usual way in the almanac's daily pages and increment tables. Figure 10–7 shows a tabular GHA Aries at 23ʰ GMT on March 16 of 159°42.5′, and Figure 10–8 shows an increment of 12°

ALTITUDE CORRECTION TABLES 10°-90°

STARS AND PLANETS				DIP				
App. Alt.	Corrⁿ	App. Alt.	Additional Corrⁿ	Ht. of Eye	Corrⁿ	Ht. of Eye	Ht. of Eye	Corrⁿ
° ′	′			m	′	ft.	m	′
9 56			1984	2·4		8·0	1·0 —	1·8
	−5·3		VENUS		−2·8			
10 08				2·6		8·6	1·5 —	2·2
	−5·2				−2·9			
10 20			Jan. 1-Dec. 12	2·8		9·2	2·0 —	2·5
	−5·1				−3·0			
10 33				3·0		9·8	2·5 —	2·8
	−5·0	°	′		−3·1			
10 46		0	+ 0·1	3·2		10·5	3·0 —	3·0
	−4·9	60			−3·2			
	−2·4	41	+ 0·1	10·3	−5·7	33·9	8 —	2·7
22 19		76		10·6		35·1	10 —	3·1
	−2·3				−5·8			
23 13			Aug. 28-Dec. 31	11·0		36·3	See table	
	−2·2				−5·9			
24 11				11·4		37·6	←	
	−2·1	°	′		−6·0			
25 14		0	+ 0·1	11·8		38·9		
	−2·0	60			−6·1			
26 22				12·2		40·1	ft.	′
	−1·9				−6·2			
27 36				12·6		41·5	70 —	8·1
	−1·8				−6·3			
28 56				13·0		42·8	75 —	8·4
	−1·7				−6·4			
30 24				13·4		44·2	80 —	8·7
	−1·6				−6·5			

Figure 10–6. **Excerpt from the *Nautical Almanac*'s altitude correction tables showing a dip correction of –2.9′ for a height of eye of 9 feet, and an R-correction of –1.9′ for a star altitude of 27°11.5′**

1984 MARCH 16

	G.M.T.	ARIES G.H.A.
	h	° ′
16	00	173 45.8
	01	188 48.3
	02	203 50.8
	03	218 53.2
	04	233 55.7
	05	248 58.2
	06	264 00.6
	07	279 03.1
	08	294 05.5
F	09	309 08.0
R	10	324 10.5
I	11	339 12.9
D	12	354 15.4
A	13	9 17.9
Y	14	24 20.3
	15	39 22.8
	16	54 25.3
	17	69 27.7
	18	84 30.2
	19	99 32.7
	20	114 35.1
	21	129 37.6
	22	144 40.0
	23	159 42.5

Figure 10–7. Excerpt from the *Nautical Almanac*'s daily pages showing GHA Aries at 23h on March 16, 1984, to be 159°42.5′

INCREMENTS AND CORRECTIONS 51m

m 51	SUN PLANETS	ARIES	MOON	v or d	Corrn	v or d	Corrn	v or d	Corrn
s	° ′	° ′	° ′	′	′	′	′	′	′
00	12 45·0	12 47·1	12 10·2	0·0	0·0	6·0	5·2	12·0	10·3
01	12 45·3	12 47·3	12 10·4	0·1	0·1	6·1	5·2	12·1	10·4
02	12 45·5	12 47·6	12 10·6	0·2	0·2	6·2	5·3	12·2	10·5
03	12 45·8	12 47·8	12 10·9	0·3	0·3	6·3	5·4	12·3	10·6
04	12 46·0	12 48·1	12 11·1	0·4	0·3	6·4	5·5	12·4	10·6
05	12 46·3	12 48·3	12 11·3	0·5	0·4	6·5	5·6	12·5	10·7
06	12 46·5	12 48·6	12 11·6	0·6	0·5	6·6	5·7	12·6	10·8
07	12 46·8	12 48·8	12 11·8	0·7	0·6	6·7	5·8	12·7	10·9
08	12 47·0	12 49·1	12 12·1	0·8	0·7	6·8	5·8	12·8	11·0
09	12 47·3	12 49·4	12 12·3	0·9	0·8	6·9	5·9	12·9	11·1

Figure 10–8. Excerpt from the *Nautical Almanac*'s *Increments and Corrections* tables showing the GHA increment for Aries to be 12°49.4′ for 51 minutes, 09 seconds of time

49.4′ for 51 minutes and 09 seconds of time. The sum of the two is the GHA Aries at 23:51:09, 172°31.9′. Applying the estimated longitude of 79°31.9′W (remembering to add if East and subtract if West), the local hour angle of Aries works out to a convenient 93°. Because the longitude is a determining factor in the accuracy of the Polaris procedure, you should always use your best estimate, even if LHA ♈ comes out to fractional degrees.

Having found the local hour angle of Aries, turn to the special Polaris tables in the back of the *Nautical Almanac*, Figure 10–9, to find the three corrections to the observed altitude which will produce the latitude. Entering the upper part of the table with the LHA ♈ of 93°, the first correction, a_0 is found to be 34.3′. The second correction, a_1, depends on the latitude; here, using the same column, it is 0.4′ for our estimated position between 26° and 27°N. The third correction, a_2, is a function of the month; in March 1984, the correction is 0.9′. The formula for calculating latitude is:

$$\text{Latitude} = \text{Ho} - 1° + a_0 + a_1 + a_2$$

If you follow the final four entries on the workform, you will see that the total adjustment nets out to –24.4′, which, when applied to the observed altitude of 27°09.6′, produces the observer's latitude, 26°45.2′, or some four miles north of the navigator's estimated position.

If you prefer, and are using Pub. No. 249, Volume I, for your star sights, the Polaris corrections can also be obtained by a single entry of LHA ♈ in Table 6, illustrated in Figure 10–10. Here you will see that for 93° the correction is –25′, very close to the net of the *Nautical Almanac* table, although the latter is usually the more accurate.

Latitude is not the only useful determination that can

Figure 10–9. **Polaris tables from the *Nautical Almanac*. Used for the determination of latitude by an observation of Polaris.**

POLARIS (POLE STAR) TABLES, 1984

FOR DETERMINING LATITUDE FROM SEXTANT ALTITUDE AND FOR AZIMUTH

L.H.A. ARIES	0°–9°	10°–19°	20°–29°	30°–39°	40°–49°	50°–59°	60°–69°	70°–79°	80°–89°	90°–99°	100°–109°	110°–119°
	a_0	a_0	a_0	a_0	a_0	a_0	a_0	a_0	a_0	a_0	a_0	a_0
°	° ′	° ′	° ′	° ′	° ′	° ′	° ′	° ′	° ′	° ′	° ′	° ′
0	0 18·8	0 14·7	0 11·9	0 10·6	0 10·8	0 12·4	0 15·5	0 19·9	0 25·5	0 32·2	0 39·6	0 47·6
1	18·3	14·4	11·7	10·6	10·9	12·7	15·9	20·4	26·2	32·9	40·4	48·4
2	17·9	14·0	11·5	10·5	11·0	12·9	16·3	21·0	26·8	33·6	41·2	49·3
3	17·4	13·7	11·4	10·5	11·1	13·2	16·7	21·5	27·4	34·3	42·0	50·1
4	17·0	13·4	11·2	10·5	11·3	13·5	17·1	22·0	28·1	35·1	42·8	50·9
5	0 16·6	0 13·1	0 11·1	0 10·5	0 11·4	0 13·8	0 17·6	0 22·6	0 28·7	0 35·8	0 43·6	0 51·8
6	16·2	12·9	11·0	10·5	11·6	14·1	18·0	23·2	29·4	36·6	44·4	52·6
7	15·8	12·6	10·9	10·6	11·8	14·5	18·5	23·8	30·1	37·3	45·2	53·4
8	15·4	12·4	10·8	10·6	12·0	14·8	19·0	24·3	30·8	38·1	46·0	54·3
9	15·0	12·1	10·7	10·7	12·2	15·2	19·4	24·9	31·5	38·8	46·8	55·1
10	0 14·7	0 11·9	0 10·6	0 10·8	0 12·4	0 15·5	0 19·9	0 25·5	0 32·2	0 39·6	0 47·6	0 56·0
Lat.	a_1	a_1	a_1	a_1	a_1	a_1	a_1	a_1	a_1	a_1	a_1	a_1
°	′	′	′	′	′	′	′	′	′	′	′	′
0	0·5	0·6	0·6	0·6	0·6	0·5	0·5	0·4	0·4	0·3	0·2	0·2
10	·5	·6	·6	·6	·6	·6	·5	·5	·4	·3	·3	·3
20	·5	·6	·6	·6	·6	·6	·5	·5	·4	·4	·3	·3
30	·6	·6	·6	·6	·6	·6	·5	·5	·5	·4	·4	·4
40	0·6	0·6	0·6	0·6	0·6	0·6	0·6	0·5	0·5	0·5	0·5	0·5
45	·6	·6	·6	·6	·6	·6	·6	·6	·6	·6	·5	·5
50	·6	·6	·6	·6	·6	·6	·6	·6	·6	·6	·6	·6
55	·6	·6	·6	·6	·6	·6	·6	·6	·6	·7	·7	·7
60	·6	·6	·6	·6	·6	·6	·6	·7	·7	·7	·8	·8
62	0·7	0·6	0·6	0·6	0·6	0·6	0·7	0·7	0·7	0·8	0·8	0·8
64	·7	·6	·6	·6	·6	·6	·7	·7	·8	·8	·9	·9
66	·7	·6	·6	·6	·6	·6	·7	·8	·8	·9	0·9	0·9
68	0·7	0·6	0·6	0·6	0·6	0·7	0·7	0·8	0·9	0·9	1·0	1·0
Month	a_2	a_2	a_2	a_2	a_2	a_2	a_2	a_2	a_2	a_2	a_2	a_2
	′	′	′	′	′	′	′	′	′	′	′	′
Jan.	0·7	0·7	0·7	0·7	0·7	0·7	0·7	0·7	0·7	0·7	0·6	0·6
Feb.	·6	·6	·7	·7	·7	·7	·8	·8	·8	·8	·8	·8
Mar.	·5	·5	·6	·6	·7	·7	·8	·8	·8	·9	·9	·9
Apr.	0·3	0·4	0·4	0·5	0·5	0·6	0·7	0·7	0·8	0·9	0·9	0·9
May	·2	·2	·3	·3	·4	·5	·5	·6	·7	·8	·8	·9
June	·2	·2	·2	·2	·3	·3	·4	·5	·5	·6	·7	·8
July	0·2	0·2	0·2	0·2	0·2	0·3	0·3	0·3	0·4	0·5	0·5	0·6
Aug.	·4	·3	·3	·3	·3	·2	·3	·3	·3	·3	·4	·4
Sept.	·5	·5	·4	·4	·3	·3	·3	·3	·3	·3	·3	·3
Oct.	0·7	0·7	0·6	0·5	0·5	0·4	0·4	0·3	0·3	0·3	0·3	0·3
Nov.	0·9	0·9	0·8	·7	·7	·6	·5	·5	·4	·4	·3	·3
Dec.	1·0	1·0	1·0	0·9	0·8	0·8	0·7	0·6	0·6	0·5	0·4	0·4
Lat.	AZIMUTH											
°	°	°	°	°	°	°	°	°	°	°	°	°
0	0·4	0·3	0·1	0·0	359·8	359·7	359·6	359·5	359·4	359·3	359·2	359·2
20	0·4	0·3	0·1	0·0	359·8	359·7	359·6	359·4	359·3	359·2	359·2	359·2
40	0·5	0·3	0·2	0·0	359·8	359·6	359·5	359·3	359·2	359·1	359·0	359·0
50	0·6	0·4	0·2	0·0	359·8	359·5	359·3	359·2	359·0	358·9	358·8	358·8
55	0·7	0·5	0·2	0·0	359·7	359·5	359·3	359·1	358·9	358·8	358·7	358·6
60	0·8	0·5	0·3	0·0	359·7	359·4	359·1	358·9	358·7	358·6	358·5	358·4
65	0·9	0·6	0·3	0·0	359·6	359·3	359·0	358·7	358·5	358·3	358·2	358·1

Latitude = Apparent altitude (corrected for refraction) − 1° + a_0 + a_1 + a_2

The table is entered with L.H.A. Aries to determine the column to be used; each column refers to a ange of 10°. a_0 is taken, with mental interpolation, from the upper table with the units of L.H.A. Aries in legrees as argument; a_1, a_2 are taken, without interpolation, from the second and third tables with arguments atitude and month respectively. a_0, a_1, a_2 are always positive. The final table gives the azimuth of *Polaris.*

TABLE 6—CORRECTION (*Q*) FOR *POLARIS*

LHA ♈	*Q*	LHA ♈	*Q*	LHA ♈	*Q*	LHA ♈	*Q*	LHA ♈	*Q*	LHA ♈	*Q*	LHA ♈	*Q*	LHA ♈
° ′	′	° ′	′	° ′	′	° ′	′	° ′	′	° ′	′	° ′	′	°
359 40		84 18		118 16		150 19		205 44		276 27		308 39		342 1
	−40		−30		−4		22		+48		+22		4	
1 49		85 49		119 28		151 40		222 23		277 48		309 51		343 4
	−41		−29		3		23		+47		+21		−5	
4 06		87 18		120 40		153 02		228 31		279 08		311 03		345 2
	−42		−28		2		24		+46		20		−6	
6 33		88 46		121 52		154 25		232 45		280 27		312 15		346 5
	−43		−27		1		25		+45		19		−7	
9 14		90 13		123 03		155 49		236 13		281 45		313 27		348 3
	−44		−26		0		26		+44		18		8	
12 12		91 37		124 16		157 14		239 14		283 03		314 40		350 1
	−45		−25		1		27		+43		17		9	
15 37		93 01		125 27		158 41		241 56		284 19		315 52		352 0
	46		−24		2		28		42		16		10	
19 48		94 23		126 39		160 10		244 25		285 35		317 06		353 5
	47		−23		3		29		41		15		11	
25 51		95 45		127 51		161 40		246 44		286 51		318 19		355 4
	48		−22		4		30		40		14		−12	
42 16		97 05		129 03		163 12		248 54		288 06		319 33		357 3
	47		21		5		31		39		13		13	
48 19		98 24		130 15		164 47		250 58		289 21		320 47		359 4
	46		20		6		32		38		12		−14	
52 30		99 43		131 27		166 23		252 56		290 35		322 02		1 4
	45		19		7		33		37		11		15	
55 55		101 01		132 40		168 02		254 49		291 48		323 17		4 0
	44		18		8		34		36		10		16	
58 53		102 18		133 52		169 44		256 38		293 02		324 33		6 3
	43		17		9		35		35		9		17	
61 34		103 34		135 05		171 29		258 23		294 15		325 49		9 1
	42		−16		10		36		34		8		18	
64 01		104 50		136 19		173 18		260 05		295 27		327 06		12 1
	41		−15		11		37		33		7		19	
66 18		106 05		137 32		175 11		261 44		296 40		328 24		15 3
	40		−14		12		38		32		6		20	
68 27		107 20		138 46		177 09		263 20		297 52		329 43		19 4
	39		−13		13		39		31		5		21	
70 29		108 34		140 01		179 13		264 55		299 04		331 02		25 5
	38		12		14		40		30		4		22	
72 26		109 48		141 16		181 23		266 27		300 16		332 22		42 1
	37		11		15		41		29		3		23	
74 17		111 01		142 32		183 42		267 57		301 28		333 44		48 1
	36		10		16		42		28		2		24	
76 05		112 15		143 48		186 11		269 26		302 40		335 06		52 3
	35		9		17		43		27		1		25	
77 49		113 27		145 04		188 53		270 53		303 51		336 30		55 5
	34		8		18		44		26		0		26	
79 30		114 40		146 22		191 54		272 18		305 04		337 54		58 5
	33		7		19		45		25		1		27	
81 08		115 52		147 40		195 22		273 42		306 15		339 21		61 3
	32		6		20		46		24		2		28	
82 44		117 04		148 59		199 36		275 05		307 27		340 49		64 0
	31		5		21		47		23		3		29	
84 18		118 16		150 19		205 44		276 27		308 39		342 18		66 1

The above table, which does *not* include refraction, gives the quantity *Q* to be applied to the corrected sextant alti[tude of] *Polaris* to give the latitude of the observer. In critical cases ascend.

Polaris: Mag. 2·1, SHA 325 56′, Dec. N 89 12′·0

TABLE 7—AZIMUTH OF *POLARIS*

LHA ♈	Latitude 0	30	50	55	60	65	70	LHA ♈	Latitude 0	30	50	55	60	65
0	0·4	0·5	0·7	0·8	0·9	1·1	1·4	180	359·6	359·5	359·3	359·2	359·1	359·0
10	0·3	0·4	0·5	0·6	0·7	0·8	1·0	190	359·7	359·6	359·5	359·4	359·4	359·2
20	0·2	0·2	0·3	0·3	0·4	0·5	0·6	200	359·8	359·8	359·7	359·7	359·6	359·6
30	0·1	0·1	0·1	0·1	0·1	0·1	0·2	210	359·9	359·9	359·9	359·9	359·9	359·9
40	359·9	359·9	359·9	359·9	359·8	359·8	359·7	220	0·1	0·1	0·1	0·1	0·2	0·2
50	359·8	359·7	359·7	359·6	359·6	359·5	359·3	230	0·2	0·3	0·3	0·4	0·4	0·5
60	359·7	359·6	359·4	359·4	359·3	359·1	358·9	240	0·3	0·4	0·5	0·6	0·7	0·8
70	359·5	359·5	359·3	359·2	359·0	358·9	358·6	250	0·5	0·5	0·7	0·8	0·9	1·1
80	359·4	359·3	359·1	359·0	358·8	358·6	358·3	260	0·6	0·7	0·9	1·0	1·1	1·3
90	359·3	359·2	359·0	358·8	358·7	358·4	358·0	270	0·7	0·8	1·0	1·1	1·3	1·5
100	359·3	359·2	358·9	358·7	358·5	358·3	357·8	280	0·7	0·8	1·1	1·3	1·4	1·7
110	359·2	359·1	358·8	358·6	358·4	358·2	357·7	290	0·8	0·9	1·2	1·3	1·5	1·8
120	359·2	359·1	358·8	358·6	358·4	358·1	357·7	300	0·8	0·9	1·2	1·4	1·6	1·9
130	359·2	359·1	358·8	358·6	358·4	358·1	357·7	310	0·8	0·9	1·2	1·4	1·6	1·9
140	359·2	359·1	358·8	358·7	358·5	358·2	357·8	320	0·8	0·9	1·2	1·3	1·5	1·8
150	359·3	359·2	358·9	358·8	358·6	358·3	357·9	330	0·7	0·8	1·1	1·3	1·5	1·7
160	359·4	359·3	359·0	358·9	358·7	358·5	358·1	340	0·6	0·8	1·0	1·1	1·3	1·6
170	359·4	359·4	359·1	359·0	358·9	358·7	358·4	350	0·6	0·6	0·9	1·0	1·1	1·3
180	359·6	359·5	359·3	359·2	359·1	359·0	358·7	360	0·4	0·5	0·7	0·8	0·9	1·1

When Cassiopeia is left (right), *Polaris* is west (east).

be made by Polaris observations; its proximity to the true pole allows accurate azimuths to be read from the same tables, and in either one you can see that the true azimuth at the time of our sight is 359.2°.

Celestial azimuths are used for comparison with the compass bearing of a body to determine compass error. Since there are no terrestrial references available at sea by which to perform a compass check, calculated azimuths are the accepted method. Besides Polaris, any celestial body can be used for the purpose—the sun is actually the most common one—and the azimuth is determined by a regular sight reduction. If you only want the azimuth, however, you need not bother with the sextant observation; all you need is the local hour angle at the time you take the bearing of a body, its declination, and your assumed latitude to enter the sight reduction tables and extract the true azimuth.

Before concluding the subject of sight reduction by tables, it is useful to compare the six types of sights we have discussed in the preceding chapters—sun, moon, planets, stars, LAN sun, and Polaris—and to review the similarities and differences in the procedures for dealing with each. Since most of the steps are similar in each instance, navigators find it easiest to remember one general procedure, and to think of the small differences as exceptions peculiar to a certain type of observation. The table on pages 94–95 shows each of the headings used in a standard sight reduction, the source of the information needed, and for each type of sight, the measurement involved. The Appendix contains standardized workbook forms for each of the procedures, and with these tools, the almanac, and Pub. No. 249, you should be able to solve any sight you take.

***Figure 10–10.* Tables 6 and 7 from Pub. No. 249, Volume I, showing the "Q" correction for LHA ♈ 93° to be –25′. The true azimuth is 359.2°.**

COMPARISON OF PROCE

VALUE SOUGHT	SOURCE	SUN	MOON
hs	Sextant	Lower or Upper Limb	Lower or Upp
IC	Measurement	Pretrial	Pretria
D	Dip table	Almanac, front cover	Almanac, bac
ha	Calculation	hs + IC + D	hs + IC
R	Almanac table	Front cover, SUN column	Back cov two parts:
Ho	Calculation	ha + R	ha + R +
GMT	Watch (+ZD)	Greenwich mean time	Greenw mean ti
gha^h	Almanac daily pages	SUN column, hours	MOON col hours
incr^{ms}	Increments & corrections tables	SUN column, min., sec.	MOON co min., s
add'l corr	Increments & corrections tables	(none required)	$\underline{\lambda}$-Correc
GHA	Calculation	gha + incr	gha + incr +
$\underline{a}\lambda$	Assumed	Near DR, to make LHA whole degree	Near DR, to LHA whole
LHA	Calculation	GHA + $\underline{a}\lambda$	GHA +
Dec	Almanac daily pages	SUN column, interpol.	MOON co + $\underline{d}$ co
$\underline{a}$L	Assumed	Whole degree near DR	Whole de near D
Tab Hc	Pub. No. 249	Vol. II/III	Vol. II/
Corr	Pub. No. 249	Table 5	Table
Hc	Calculation	Tab Hc + corr	Tab Hc +
Ho	Earlier calculation	(From above)	(From ab
a	Calculation	Ho − Hc	Ho −
Zn	Pub. No. 249	Z + rules	Z + ru

(Note: Plus sign indicates algebraic sum; minus sign indicates take differe

ELESTIAL OBSERVATIONS

LANETS	STARS	LAN-SUN	POLARIS
ter of disc	Center light source	Lower limb—Max. altitude	Center light source
Pretrial	Pretrial	Pretrial	Pretrial
ac, front cover	Almanac, front cover	Almanac, front cover	Almanac, front cover
+ IC + D	hs + IC + D	hs + IC + D	hs + IC + D
nt cover, ET columns	Front cover, STAR column	Front cover, SUN column	Front cover, STAR column
a + R	ha + R	ha + R	ha + R
eenwich ean time	Greenwich mean time	Max. altitude; approx. Greenwich mean time	Greenwich mean time
of PLANET mn, hours	ARIES column, hours	(not required)	ARIES column, hours
TS column, in., sec.	ARIES column, min., sec.	(not required)	ARIES column, min., sec.
orrection	SHA★ (Vol. II/III)	(not required)	(not required)
ncr + $\underline{\lambda}$-Corr.	gha + incr (+ SHA★)	(not required)	gha + incr
R, to make hole degree	Near DR, to make LHA whole degree	(not required except for estimating time of LAN)	Best estimate of present longitude
+ $\underline{a}\lambda$	GHA + $\underline{a}\lambda$	(not required)	GHA + est. λ
ET column $\underline{d}$ corr.	Almanac STAR list	SUN column, interpol.	(not required)
le degree ear DR	Whole degree near DR	(not required)	Best estimate of present latitude
l. II/III	Vol. I, II, or III	(not required)	(not required, use Polaris table)
able 5	Vol. I—not required Vol. II/III—Table 5	(not required)	(not required)
c + Corr.	Vol. I—read directly Vol. II/III—Tab Hc + corr.	(not required)	(not required)
n above)	(From above)	Calculate latitude	Calculate latitude
— Hc	Ho — Hc	Read latitude	Read latitude
+ rules	Vol. I—read directly Vol. II/III—Z + rules	North or South	Polaris table

11 Celestial Theory

In the introductory remarks, I proposed to concentrate first on the practical technique, leaving celestial theory until later. Having done so, let's look now at some of the underlying mechanics involved in modern celestial navigation. In a century which has seen the development of electric light, the automobile, air travel, and even space exploration, it is remarkable that celestial navigation, except for timekeeping, has changed only by refinement since its last major breakthrough—the discovery, in 1837, of the line-of-position concept by an American captain, Thomas Sumner, and the altitude-intercept method of computation developed a few years later by a French commander, Marcq St.-Hilaire. This is not to suggest that the science has been allowed to become obsolete; on the contrary, the methods have withstood the test of time.

Each of the regular celestial procedures described in the preceding chapters is comprised of three key operations, identified for the sake of simplicity as, "shoot," "compute," and "compare." "Shoot" refers to the measurement of the altitude of a celestial body with a precision instrument such as a marine sextant. In concept, the measurement is of the angle between the true horizontal and a line from the center of the earth to the celestial body, but in practice, the measurement is of the angle between the line of sight to the visible horizon and the line of sight from the observer to the body, and it is made from a position on the earth's surface. As a result, adjustments have to be made to the measured altitude in order to arrive at the true altitude desired.

The normal altitude corrections are the three seen in each of our practical examples: an adjustment for instrument error (the index correction), primarily due to lack of parallelism of the index and horizon mirrors; an adjustment for the observer's elevated position, which causes the visible horizon to appear below the true horizontal (the dip correction); and an adjustment to compensate for the bending of light rays as they pass through the earth's atmosphere (the refraction correction). In the case of the moon, an additional adjustment is needed for parallax—the difference in the body's apparent position as viewed from the surface instead of from the center of the earth. All the other celestial bodies are so far distant from the earth that the parallax correction is negligible, and the few other minor adjustments that might apply are incorporated in the almanac tables. After correction, the sextant altitude becomes the true, or "observed" altitude, Ho, and is the value used in the subsequent calculations.

Turning to celestial mechanics, at any moment in time there is a single point on the earth's surface that is directly beneath a given celestial body. Known, variously, as the subsolar, sublunar, or substellar point, depending upon the body observed, the point is commonly referred to as the body's geographical position, or GP. It is the one location where the body, at that particular moment, is at the zenith—vertically overhead. In piloting, you learned that if you can locate a point precisely, and can determine your distance from it, your position must be somewhere on the circumference of the circle whose center is at the designated point, and whose radius is your distance from it. At the same time, if you know your exact direction from the point, you know where you are on the circumference. In celestial navigation, we can determine the precise location of a body's geographical position by means of the almanac, and can determine our distance from that GP by our altitude measurement, as will be explained in a moment. The problem, however, is that the distance, though accurate, is usually so great that it is not practical to plot the circle of position; and shipboard bearing-measurements are not precise enough to be able to pinpoint your location on it. As a consequence, St.-Hilaire's indirect method of approach was developed.

Visualize, if you will, the right angle formed at the geographical position of a body, between the horizontal line to the observer and the perpendicular line to the body, and you can see that it is but one element of a right triangle whose three points are the observer, the GP, and the body at the zenith. The outermost triangle in Figure 11–1 illustrates the relationship. The second angle of the right triangle is the altitude of the body as measured at the observer's position (angle Ho in the figure), and the third is the angle formed at the zenith. Because the triangle is a right triangle, the third angle is the complement of the second, and for this reason, it is known as the coaltitude (90°– altitude). In the figure, you can also see that the coaltitude is subtended by the line between the GP and the observer, and it is a measure of the angular distance (arc distance) between the two points. For this reason, the coaltitude is often referred to as the zenith distance, although "zenith angle" might be more descriptive and less confusing.

For any given angle at the zenith (or for the altitude angle that complements it), the locus of all points on

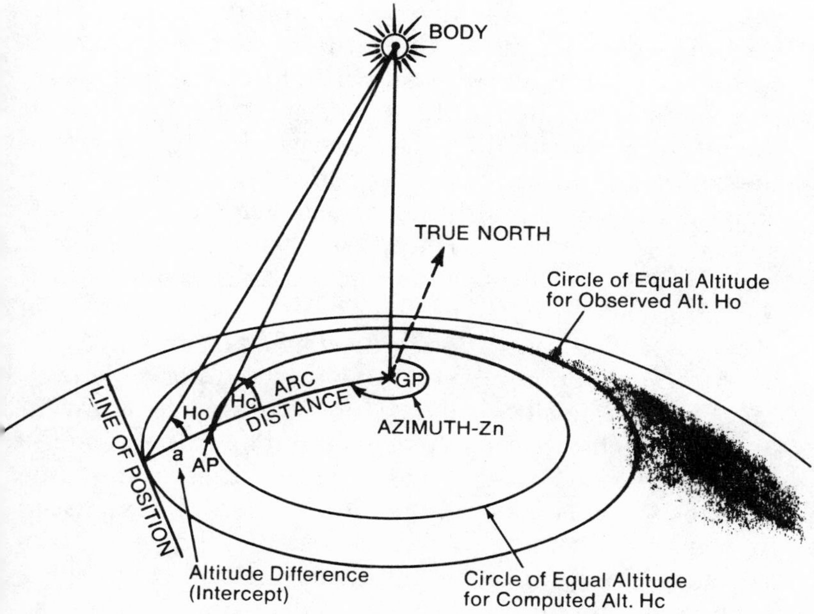

***Figure 11–1.* Elements of the horizon system, showing how the difference between the observed altitude, Ho, and the computed altitude, Hc, establishes the intercept, a.**

earth where the angle remains the same is the circle, previously mentioned, whose center is the GP, and whose radius is the distance between the GP and the point from which the altitude is measured. This circle, illustrated in Figure 11–1, is called a circle of equal altitude—everywhere on its circumference, the altitude of the celestial body will be the same. As I have explained, even though we can find the information necessary to describe the circle of equal altitude for a given observation, it usually isn't practical to plot it because the circle is so large. The alternative, then, is to "compute," St.-Hilaire's ingenious idea of constructing a simultaneous, second circle of equal altitude from a *known* position (the assumed position, AP) by computing the altitude of the body as it would be at the assumed position. In the final, "compare" phase, that computed altitude, Hc, can be compared with the altitude measured by the observer, Ho, to determine the difference in arc distance from the GP between the actual and assumed altitude circles. The altitude difference is the intercept, a, shown in Figure 11–1, and you can also see that if the computed altitude is greater than the observed altitude, as it appears in the figure, the observer's position will be farthest away from the GP.

Although you know now how far the observer is from the assumed position, it is still necessary to know in exactly which direction. This is found by calculating the bearing of the GP from the assumed position at the same time the altitude is computed. That direction, expressed in compass degrees from true North, is known as the azimuth, Zn. While the intercept method adopts the convention that the same azimuth will apply to the bearing of the GP from the observer's actual position, it is not exactly true, but since the positions are so close in global terms, any small difference is immaterial.

As you can see in Figure 11–1, the intersection of the azimuth line with the observer's circle of equal altitude identifies the portion of the circumference on which the observer is located. Because the circumference is usually so large, and since the azimuth may not be exact, for the reason explained, the line of position is constructed as a short, straight line at right angles to the azimuth at the point of intersection. It is virtually coincident with the circumference, and for practical purposes, the line can be used just as is any other line of position.

In discussing the "compute" phase, we passed over the technique of making the actual calculation of the computed altitude and azimuth. It employs the methods of trigonometry, and you may recall, if you have ever studied the subject, that if you are given certain parts—sides and angles—of triangles, you can, by using established formulas, find the missing elements. The same concept applies to a triangle on a sphere, as well as to one on a plane surface, and it is a spherical triangle that is used in celestial navigation. Appropriately named the navigational triangle, its various elements are illustrated in Figure 11–2.

For computing the altitude and azimuth from an assumed position, we predetermine two of the sides, the polar distance (90° minus the body's declination) and the colatitude (90° minus the assumed latitude), and the included angle, the local hour angle, LHA. The triangle is then solved for the third side, the coaltitude, and its adjacent angle, the azimuth angle, Z. The first side, polar distance, is obtained by finding the body's declination in the almanac for the time of the observation, and subtract-

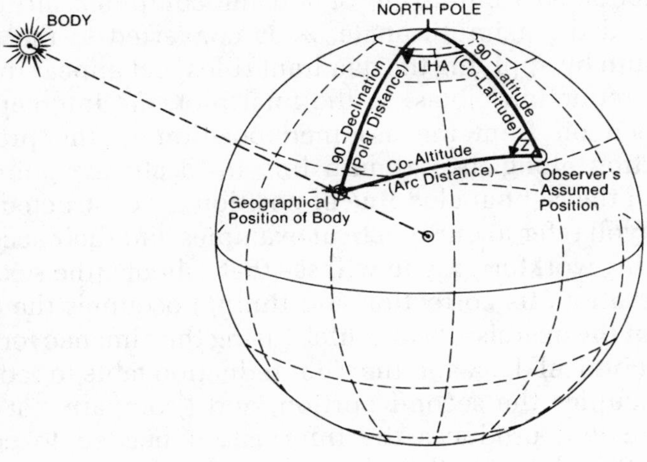

Figure 11–2. **The Elements of the Navigational Triangle Projected on Earth**

ing that value from 90°. The colatitude is determined directly by subtracting the latitude of the assumed position from 90°. The local hour angle is found by applying the longitude of the assumed position to the Greenwich hour angle of the body from the almanac. The relationship between Greenwich hour angle, local hour angle, and longitude has been explained in Chapter 3, and is illustrated in Figure 3–1.

While the methods of spherical trigonometry are used in the solution, the manual computation is tedious, and two alternatives are available to the modern navigator: the use of inspection tables, such as Pub. No. 249, recommended in this book; and by means of an electronic calculator, discussed in Chapter 12. The process, however worked, is called sight reduction, and the special tables for the purpose are known as sight reduction tables.

Once the missing elements of the navigational triangle have been found, the side identified as the coaltitude is subtracted from 90° to obtain the computed altitude, Hc, and the azimuth angle, Z, is converted to the true azimuth by applying the quadrant rules that appear in the sight reduction tables. In the final plot, the intercept is stepped off from the assumed position in the proper direction along the azimuth line to locate the point at which the right-angled line of position is constructed.

If you refer to our practical examples and their accompanying workforms, you will see that "shoot" (the sextant observation, its correction and timing) occupies the first part of the exercise; "compute" (using the almanac for the astronomical data, and the sight reduction table to reduce it) occupies the second portion; and "compare," at the conclusion, produces the information needed to complete the plot. Whether or not you become a student of celestial theory, "shoot," "compute," and "compare" will help you to remember the routine, and a well-rehearsed routine is the very best way to avoid mistakes.

12 Celestial Navigation by Calculator

The principal procedures in celestial navigation, as in mathematical sciences generally, are able to be expressed in numerical terms, and the solutions to them obtained by the application of conventional mathematical precepts. Historically, however, mathematical solutions have been avoided by practicing navigators, because of the tedious computations involved and the inherent opportunity for error. The advent of the electronic calculator has had an effect on this posture, since it is now possible to deal rapidly and accurately with quite complex computations. As a result, it is not unusual to find a calculator as part of a modern navigator's kit.

For discussion purposes, the celestial procedure can be divided into three categories: *arithmetic operations,* normally performed by hand, exemplified by the correction process for sextant altitudes; *astronomical calculations,* normally extracted from the almanac, which are based on long and complex formulas; and *sight reductions,* usually resolved by means of sight reduction tables, which are straightforward exercises in spherical trigonometry.

How each operational category is handled by calculator is largely a function of the type of calculator used. While terminology in the industry is not yet standardized, the "scientific," or "slide-rule" designation has come to describe that class of calculators, next above the four-function arithmetic variety, which provide additional, scientifically oriented functions, such as raising to powers and extracting roots, and the natural trigonometric functions and their inverses. Most calculators in this category also provide a wide range of other higher-level functions; some of these functions, such as multiple memories and coordinate-conversion capabilities, are particularly useful to navigators.

A manual, scientific-level calculator represents the minimum calculator for practical celestial navigation, but with manual operation, there is little time to be saved against that of an experienced navigator using modern inspection tables like the *Nautical Almanac* and Pub. No. 249. For that reason, if a calculator is to be used regulary for celestial navigation, most navigators prefer the more advanced, programmable types. General-purpose, scientific-level, programmable calculators, such as the Hewlett-Packard Series 40, not only have the capability to be programmed by the operator, but they can also accept modular memories which have been preprogrammed by the manufacturer to perform a variety of procedures, including celestial navigation. Specialized navigational calculators are another class which has found favor with yacht navigators. These instruments, exemplified by the Tamaya NC series, are prewired specifically to perform navigational computations. Since this is their primary purpose, they are called dedicated, or hard-wired calculators, and their keyboards and displays are all designed to facilitate navigation solutions. These two types of dedicated instruments are both capable of a complete celestial solution, with the operator supplying only the raw data as input. For yachtsmen who use celestial navigation only occasionally, the specialized navigation calculator will probably be the easiest and most convenient to use, but for navigators who wish to make a variety of other types of calculations on a regular basis, the general-purpose calculators, with specialized modules, are the logical choice.

In essence, a calculator accepts input data in a predetermined order, and through a stepped sequence—executed either by a series of individual key strokes in a manual machine, or automatically in a programmed model—arrives at the solution. The formula to be applied determines the steps in the sequence. If an operator develops the sequence, he must store it in the program memory before entering the variable data and running the program; in the case of the dedicated instruments and modules, the program has already been established by the manufacturer, and the operator need only enter the input and command the machine to execute. The technique of programming a particular calculator is a function of the model and its design, but any program involves identifying the input information available, the output solution desired, and the formula which will be applied. It is an absorbing exercise if one is mathematically inclined, but it does require knowledge of both the mathematical basis of the problem and the machine's programming procedure, and, if you are to be good at it, lots of practice.

Let's review the principal celestial operations that we have studied in earlier chapters, and look at the approach to solving them by calculator. The first category includes the process of finding and applying the regular corrections to the sextant altitude. The index correction, you will recall, is found by trial, while the dip and refraction corrections are normally extracted from the almanac tables. The last two corrections can also be calculated. The formula for finding dip correction, in minutes of arc, is:

$$0.97\sqrt{\text{Height of eye (in feet)}}$$

and the formula for finding the refraction correction, in decimal degrees, where the apparent altitude, ha, is given in decimal degrees is:

$$\frac{0.97 \tan[\text{ha} - \tan^{-1} 12(\text{ha} + 3)]}{60}$$

You will notice that the last formula is expressed in decimal degrees, while the first formula and the index correction normally use minutes of arc. Therefore, in determining the algebraic sum by calculator, it is necessary to express all the values in the same terms—decimal degrees—perform the arithmetic, and then reconvert the total to the sexagesimal system (60 seconds equals 1 minute, and 60 minutes equals 1 degree), the way in which navigators usually state angular measurement. On certain calculators, the conversion function is programmed into the instrument, but if it is not, the formula to convert minutes and seconds of arc to decimal degrees is:

$$\frac{(\text{Minutes} \times 60) + \text{Seconds}}{3600}$$

In the case of sun or moon sights worked by calculator, an additional correction for semidiameter—it is already incorporated in the almanac's refraction tables—must be included because the formula given applies only to the center of the body. Unless the sextant corrections are performed as part of a complete celestial program, even though they are relatively easy to compute by calculator, many navigators find it just as quick to take the values from the almanac tables. The technique of performing sexagesimal/decimal conversions, then performing the addition or subtraction, and finally, returning the result to the sexagesimal system, can also be used in arithmetical routines such as finding the latitude by an observation of the sun at local apparent noon, or the latitude-by-Polaris procedure. It can be used in a similar manner to convert Greenwich hour angle to local hour angle by the application of longitude, but the process of determining the Greenwich hour angle, itself, by calculator is quite another matter.

The fundamental equations of dynamic astronomy are far too complex for direct use in the majority of applications, and even the simplified formulas used in the Naval Observatory's *Almanac for Computers* are beyond the practical reach of any manual calculator. As a consequence, the navigator has two main choices for deriving the necessary astronomical data to solve a sight. Either he can extract the data from the almanac in the conventional way, and use his calculator to combine it, or he can use one of the dedicated calculators or modules which are programmed to compute the Greenwich hour angle and declination of the celestial bodies for any moment in time. Ofttimes, these dedicated devices are capable of incorporating the astronomical data they produce in an entire celestial sequence; that is where their real time advantage appears.

Sight reduction is a much less complicated exercise in spherical trigonometry, and lends itself well to electronic calculation. There are two basic formulas that apply, in which L is the latitude, and d the declination, both expressed in decimal degrees. To find the computed altitude, Hc, in decimal degrees, the formula is:

$$\mathrm{Sin}^{-1}[(\sin L \sin d) + (\cos L \cos d \cos \mathrm{LHA})]$$

Then, the azimuth angle, Z, may be calculated from the formula:

$$\text{Cos}^{-1}\left[\frac{\sin d - (\sin L \sin \text{Hc})}{(\cos L \cos \text{Hc})}\right]$$

In both formulas, when the latitude and declination are of contrary name, declination is treated as a negative quantity.

If you try these formulas on a manual calculator, you may find, as you have in other instances, that there is not a great time saving over the use of sight reduction tables but the calculator does have one advantage over the tables: since the calculator does not require that the latitude and local hour angle be in whole degrees, the dead reckoning position may be used as the assumed position, greatly simplifying the plot.

Unless you are a calculator buff and are capable of programming your own calculator, you will probably share the conclusion of most yacht navigators that the preprogrammed instruments are the most convenient calculators for celestial navigation. Even if you decide to use one regularly, you will want to carry your almanac and sight reduction tables with you on every voyage, and *know how to use them*. The environment aboard a small boat at sea is notoriously inhospitable to delicate electronic equipment, and it would be foolhardy if, because of equipment failure, you gave up the major advantage that celestial navigation enjoys over all other offshore navigation systems: it is completely self-contained, and need be dependent only upon the navigator.

13 Practical Wrinkles

Now that you have had an opportunity to learn what celestial navigation is all about, it is time to introduce some of the practical wrinkles that experienced yacht navigators have found helpful, both in easing their burdens and improving their performance. Mine is by no means an all-inclusive list; as you gain experience yourself, you will discover a number of tricks of your own, and that is part of the pleasure to be found in the navigational art.

Planning ahead is useful in any navigational exercise, and this is particularly true in celestial navigation. One very good wrinkle, applicable to beginners and old hands alike, is to do as much preparation as possible before going on deck to take sights. This can include getting out the almanac and the appropriate volume of the sight reduction tables, checking the watch for the correct time, and in the case of star sights, preparing a list of the approximate altitudes and azimuths of the bodies you intend to shoot. If you are in an area with considerable magnetic variation, you may want to convert your azimuths to magnetic readings; it will be much easier to locate the star by the yacht's compass. It is also good practice to run up your dead reckoning position on the chart or plotting sheet, so that there will be no delay in selecting the appropriate assumed latitude and longitude when it comes time to work the sight reduction. Because the sight reduction process requires the most time in the celestial procedure, if you are planning on using visual or electronic bearings to cross with your celestial line of position, it is often advantageous to take your bearings first, so there will not be an inordinate delay between supposedly "simultaneous" lines of position. All of these preparations are designed to allow the navigator to make his observations rapidly and with a minimum of distraction, and especially, to be able to work out the sights expeditiously, without being pressured by his shipmates insistent, "You're the navigator. Where are we?"

As we have seen, the accuracy of any celestial line of position depends in large part on the accuracy of the original observation, and it is here that the navigator plays the major personal role. Anything that can contribute to improved performance is worth trying, and the simple effect of practice will improve most of your results. Some navigators get less accurate results than they should by being careless about their sextant's index error. A few professionals prefer to determine their index correction following a series of sights, but I have always found it best to get into the habit of checking it each time I go on deck and am setting up to make my observations. With a good sextant, properly cared for, the index error may change infrequently, but conditions on a small boat are never ideal for delicate equipment, and I have been surprised more than once by an unexpected change in the index error. Checking an index error takes a little practice; even the best navigators admit that they often make several tests to make sure of their findings.

Once on deck, finding a place on a small yacht from which to take sights can be a challenge. When sailing, it is often necessary to use several stations in order to avoid having the observation blanketed by the sails or interfered with by the rigging. In heavy weather, it is desirable to station yourself as high as possible above the water surface without jeopardizing your stability or safety. This is both to avoid a false horizon created by the crests of nearby seas, and to keep the sextant's optics from becoming clouded with spray. Since both hands are needed for the fine sextant adjustment, it can be helpful to hook on to the standing rigging with a safety harness, so that you can concentrate on the sight instead of fighting the motion of the boat. In any kind of a seaway, sights should be timed to take place as the vessel rises to the top of a wave, since the true horizon will also be at the distant wavetops. To overlook this point is to invite a significant error in the altitude you measure.

Earlier I explained the advantage of having a digital watch set to Greenwich mean time, and this advantage will be clearly apparent the first time you try to make an observation and take your own time from a bouncing deck. Rather than expose a fine timepiece to the elements, especially in wet conditions, I have found that a cheap, quartz wristwatch does the trick nicely, and it is only necessary to check it against an accurate timepiece once before you come on deck. If it is necessary to spend much time on deck in stormy weather, before or between sights, I have found it worthwhile to protect my sextant with a light, plastic bag. I used to use a lanyard attached to the sextant, and many navigators swear by the practice, but I found it to be one more thing to get in the way. I never let go of my sextant, nor set it down, except in its box, but even with all this care, I have succeeded in knocking it out of adjustment once or twice. If a sextant is unavoidably exposed to salt spray, it is good to remove the salt from the optical surfaces with a soft cloth dampened in fresh water. Be careful not to use coarse material, or t wipe the surfaces with a dry cloth as long as salt remains it is very easy to scratch the lens or mirror faces.

A completely overcast sky makes it impossible t obtain workable sights, but one should never give up jus because it's partly cloudy or hazy, or if the horizon i partially obscured. By lowering the height of eye as muc as practicable—I have even done this by lying on deck— your horizon is brought closer; often close enough to gai adequate definition. By use of the sextant's shades, th fuzzy image of the sun may be seen well enough throug the eyepiece to bring one limb to the horizon, eve though it doesn't appear possible to the naked eye. I broken clouds, a common condition at sea, it is a goo idea to be on deck and at the ready for that short interva when a body appears from behind a cloud, and you get of a quick shot. The three things to remember in these kind of conditions are height of eye, sextant shades, and pa tience—the latter being the test of the experienced celes tial navigator.

You have been cautioned about the potential ey damage which can occur if an index shade is not used fo sun sights, particularly on a bright, sunny day. It is rar that at least the lightest shade isn't needed for a sun sight so many careful navigators automatically swing a se lected shade into place before even starting to locate th sun's image in the horizon mirror.

In Chapter 9, we discussed some of the problems involved in taking star sights, and the same problems alsc apply to the lesser planets. At either morning or evening twilight, objects near the eastern horizon should be ob served first—in the evening, the eastern horizon darkens first, and in the morning, it becomes visible first. With al the celestial bodies, especially the planets and stars, it is desirable, when you have a choice, to concentrate on sights in the middle band of altitudes, between 15° and 70°. The problem with low-altitude sights is that the refraction is more critical, as a glance at the almanac table will confirm, and that the attenuated light passing through the earth's atmosphere at an oblique angle results in fainter images. At high altitudes, as a body approaches the zenith, it is difficult to find the point on the horizon directly beneath the observed body. When the sextant is rocked, the arc that the reflected image makes is so shallow that it is hard to determine the lowest point and to know that the sextant has been held absolutely vertically.

With regard to the horizontal dispersement of sights, you will recall that fixes resulting from lines of position which intersect at small angles are generally less reliable than those in which the angle of intersection approaches the ideal right angle. Because of this, it is preferable, whenever practical, to select bodies at 30° or greater intervals. This objective should not be carried to extremes, however; it should apply when you have a free choice. With modern equipment and extra care, the results that can be obtained from observations near the limits are far more useful than none at all.

On the matter of extremes, the altitude correction tables in the *Nautical Almanac* (Figure 1–4) are based on average conditions of temperature (50°F.) and barometric pressure (29.83 inches) at sea level. This need only concern you in cases of major deviation from these norms, and then, principally for low-altitude observations. Table A4, at the front of the almanac, provides the additional refraction correction for nonstandard conditions, but it is seldom necessary to use it in normal yachting weather.

In making stellar observations, some navigators prefer morning to evening stars, the argument being that the sea is often calmer at dawn, and since you start with all the stars visible, identification is easier. There is also an advantage in having daylight in which to work the sights after you go below, but generally speaking, if you routinely plan your round of stars in advance, and have developed an average skill in taking star sights, the difference between observations at dawn and dusk is not of great importance. The best way to identify stars is, as we have discussed, to locate them beforehand by means of Pub. No. 249 or the starfinder. In either case, you need to calculate the local hour angle of Aries, and a quick way to do this is to enter the ARIES column in the almanac's daily page, substituting your local time for Greenwich mean time, and reading the corresponding GHA Aries as LHA Aries. The local hour angle, figured this way, is only as accurate as your proximity to the standard meridian of your time zone, and the wrinkle works easiest in West longitudes, but the method is fast, and sufficiently accurate for star identification.

We have talked about thinking of the celestial procedure as a standard routine, with the minor variations required for different bodies as exceptions. One advantage in doing this is that you develop a regular pattern for using the tables. The correct page becomes easier to find in a hurry, and you are much more likely to find all the information required in a particular page opening quicker, and with less chance of error. Some navigators like to use bookmarks, or, in the almanac, to pencil out or cut off the corners of the pages as they are used.

You may recall the technique you learned in piloting for advancing lines of position to obtain a running fix. The process works equally well with celestial position lines, and it is the basis of a favorite routine of mine. The routine is to take forenoon sights of the sun, within an hour or two of local apparent noon, and to advance the resulting lines of position to LAN in order to produce a three-line, running fix. Figure 13–1 illustrates a typical morning's work. A sun sight is taken at 1100, another at 1200, and a latitude line determined at local apparent noon, at 1241. Since the vessel is traveling at 15 knots, the 1100–line is advanced an estimated 25.3 nautical miles along the course, and the 1200-line, an estimated

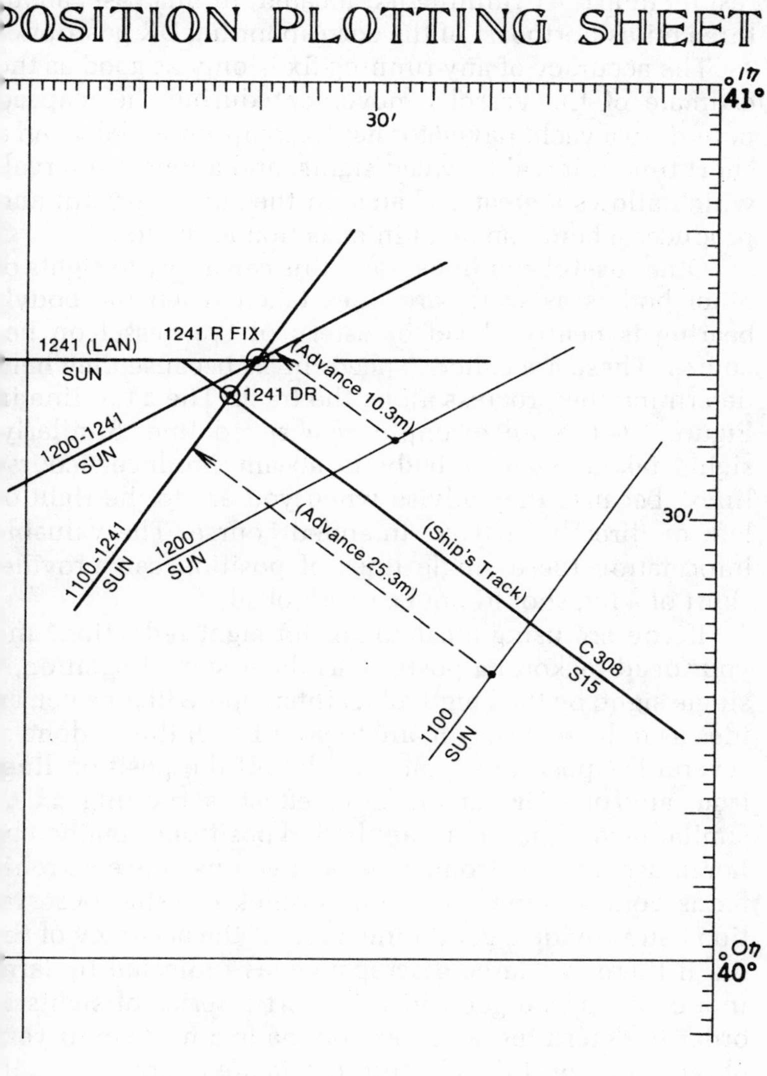

igure 13–1. **Morning sun lines, advanced and combined with a atitude observation at local apparent noon, produce a running fix.**

10.3 miles. The intersection of the three position lines results in a 1241 running fix, located, in this case, abou three miles northeast of the corresponding DR position.

The accuracy of any running fix is only as good as the estimate of the vessel's movement during the elapsed period, so a yacht navigator has to compromise between a short time interval between sights, and a longer interval which allows a greater change in the sun's azimuth and produces a better angle of intersection at the fix.

Other useful sun lines—and this can apply to sights of other bodies as well—are lines taken when the body's bearing is nearly ahead or astern of the vessel on her course. These are called "speed lines" because they help determine the progress along the track. The 1100-line in Figure 13–1 is an example of a speed line. Similarly sights taken when a body is abeam produce "course lines" because they advise when you are to the right or left, or directly on your intended course. The valuabl information these single lines of position can provide short of a fix, should not be overlooked.

If you are using a calculator for sight reduction, and your dead reckoning position as the assumed position, single sight, by the length of its intercept, will give you an idea as to how close you are to your DR. If this is done a several DR positions, you can plot all the position lines from any one DR, creating, in effect, a running fix. A similar technique can be applied to positions obtained b Loran or other electronic means. If you use the electroni fix as your assumed position, a quick celestial observa tion can provide a good indication of the accuracy of th fix. If there is a large discrepancy, as indicated by larg intercepts, it is a good idea to start a series of sights i order to determine whether you made a mistake in you observation, or if the electronic data are in error.

Two signs that are the mark of a proficient navigato are a neat, carefully labeled plot, and a well-organize workbook. There are many choices of workforms, as we have discussed, and as a guide, sample forms for the sights we have examined are included in the Appendix. Forms such as these may be combined into one universal form, although it may be a little complicated as a result; they may be prepared in pads, or in a looseleaf notebook; or placed on permanent strips, to be used as bookmarks in the margins of a blank notebook. The choice, as well as the opportunity to make improvements of your own, is up to you.

As a final bit of advice, you should know that there comes a time in every navigator's career when he is uncertain of his results, and it can happen most readily when one is fatigued. This is the time for a cool head to prevail; not the time to panic or to forge ahead blindly. Good judgment requires that you take your time, go back over your work carefully, and determine if you have made a mistake in your calculations, or whether you may have failed to follow the procedures correctly. If you are ever unsure of the procedures, it will be worthwhile to review the applicable chapters in this book, or if you are having difficulty with the tables, don't overlook the excellent explanation sections in the back of the almanac, and in the front of the sight reduction tables.

As my old Navy chief used to say after every instruction session, "When all else fails, try reading the directions."

Appendix

Navigator's Workbook

NAVIGATOR'S WORKBOOK

Sun

ATE	
DY	
rr	
MT	
a	
cr	
HA	
HA	
ec	
b. Hc	
rr	
c	
o	
n	

Lan—Sun

DATE	
Est. λ	
Std. Mer.	
Corr in time	
Mer. Pass.	
LAN	
GMT	
hs	
IC	
D	
ha	
R	
Ho	
90°	
−Ho	
z	
Dec	
L	
(name)	

NAVIGATOR'S WORKBOOK

Moon

)ATE	
3ODY	
ıs	
C	
)	
ıa	
ı.P. H. P.	
– 30′)	
ıo	
V	
orr	
MT	
ha *v*	
cr	
corr	
HA	
IA	
ec *d*	
corr	
ec	
b Hc	
rr	

Planet

DATE	
BODY	
hs	
IC	
D	
ha	
R	
add'l corr	
Ho	
W	
corr	
GMT	
gha *v*	
incr	
v corr	
GHA	
aλ	
LHA	
dec *d*	
d corr	
Dec	
a L	
Tab Hc	
corr	
Hc	
Ho	
a	
Zn	

NAVIGATOR'S WORKBOOK

Stars—Vol. I Pub. No. 249.

)ATE	
ODY	
ıs	
C	
)	
ıa	
:	
ło	
V	
orr	
;MT	
;ha ♈	
ncr	
;HA ♈	
λ	
HA ♈	
L	
łc	
ło	
:n	

Stars—Vol. II/III Pub. No. 249

DATE	
BODY	
hs	
IC	
D	
ha	
R	
Ho	
W	
corr	
GMT	
gha ♈	
incr	
GHA ♈	
SHA★	
GHA★	
a λ	
LHA★	
Dec	
a L	
Tab Hc	
corr	
Hc	
Ho	
a	
Zn	

NAVIGATOR'S WORKBOOK

Polaris

DATE	
hs	
IC	
D	
ha	
R	
Ho	
W	
corr	
GMT	
gha ♈	
incr	
GHA ♈	
a λ	
LHA ♈	
a L	
Ho	
−1°	
$+a_0$	
$+a_1$	
$+a_2$	
L	

Glossary

Almanac. A publication containing the astronomical data required for the practice of celestial navigation, arranged by calendar date and time interval. The *Nautical Almanac,* recommended in this text, supplies the information from which the Greenwich hour angle and declination of the principal celestial bodies can be determined for any instant of time.

Altitude Difference (a). The difference between the observed altitude (Ho) and the computed altitude (Hc); commonly called the intercept.

Apparent Altitude (App. Alt. or ha). The sextant altitude (hs) corrected for index error and dip.

Arc Distance. The distance measured along a curve; in celestial navigation usually a portion of a great circle.

Assumed Latitude (*a*L). The latitude at which the observer is assumed to be for the purpose of calculating the computed altitude (Hc) of a celestial body. Usually selected to the nearest whole degree.

Assumed Longitude ($a\lambda$). The longitude at which the observer is assumed to be for the purpose of calculating the computed altitude (Hc) of a celestial body. Usually selected so that the local hour angle (LHA) works out to a whole degree.

Assumed Position (AP). The position assumed for calculating the computed altitude (Hc) of a celestial body, and the point from which the altitude difference, or intercept (a) is plotted.

Azimuth (Z and Zn). The uncorrected azimuth (Z), also called azimuth angle, is measured from North (0°) or South (180°), clockwise or counterclockwise, through 180°. The corrected, or true, azimuth (Zn) is measured from North (0°) clockwise through 360°.

Celestial Sphere. An imaginary sphere, concentric with the earth and with the earth at its center, on which all the celestial bodies are presumed to be projected.

Coaltitude. 90° minus the altitude.

Computed Altitude (Hc). The altitude of a celestial body at a given time and position as determined by computation.

Critical Table. A table in which a single value is tabulated for limiting increments of entry values as, for example, the almanac's altitude correction tables.

Dead Reckoning (DR). The process of establishing a position by applying the courses and distances sailed from the last known position.

Declination (Dec or dec). The angular distance north or south of the celestial equator, corresponding to latitude on earth. The abbreviation *d* is used in the almanac to indicate the hourly change in declination.

Dip (D). The angle between the true horizon and the observer's line of sight to the visible horizon.

Equation of Time. The difference between the time of the mean sun and the apparent solar, or sundial, time. While the equation of time may be positive or negative, it never exceeds 16.4 minutes.

First Point of Aries (♈). The point at which the sun's path intersects the celestial equator as it changes from south to north declination at the Vernal Equinox. Values for the Greenwich hour angle of Aries are tabulated in the daily pages of the almanac as if it were a celestial body, and the positions of all the stars are measured westward from that point by their sidereal hour angles.

Fix. A position, determined without reference to a previous position, usually resulting from the intersection of two or more lines of position.

Geographical Position (GP). The point on earth directly beneath a celestial body.

Great Circle. The circle formed by the intersection of a plane passing through the center of a sphere with the surface of the sphere.

Greenwich Hour Angle (GHA). The angular distance measured westward from the meridian of Greenwich (0°) on the celestial sphere. Corresponds to longitude on earth. The small case abbreviation (gha) is often used to identify the uncorrected tabular value extracted from the GHA column in the almanac's daily pages.

Greenwich Mean Time (GMT). Local mean time at the meridian of Greenwich (0°). Time signals, broadcast as Coordinated Universal Time (UTC), may vary by a fraction of a second from GMT as a result of irregular rotation of the earth. For practical purposes, navigators use the two times interchangeably.

Horizon Glass. The half-mirrored glass, attached to the frame of a sextant, through which the horizon is viewed.

Horizon Shades. The darkened glass which can be moved into place to reduce the intensity of light passing through the clear portion of the horizon glass.

Horizontal Parallax (H.P.). The difference in altitude between that measured from the observer's position on the surface of the earth and that measured from the center of the earth. Of primary interest to the navigator in correcting altitudes of the moon, where the value is of significance because of the relative closeness of the moon to the earth, an additional correction for it must be taken from the almanac.

Index Arm. The movable arm of a sextant.

Index Correction (IC). The value which must be applied to correct the index error (failure to read exactly zero when the true and reflected images are in coincidence) of a sextant. Usually confirmed before or after each series of observations.

Index Shades. The darkened glass which can be moved into place between the mirror on the index arm and the eyepiece to reduce the intensity of the reflected image of a celestial body. It is essential that the reflection of the sun's image be reduced in intensity by use of the index shades since injury can result to the unprotected eye.

Inspection Tables. A volume of tabulated solutions from which an answer can be extracted by simple inspection.

Intercept (a). The difference between the observed altitude (Ho) and the computed altitude (Hc).

Interpolation. The process of determining intermediate values between given, tabular values.

Line of Position. "A line on some point of which a vessel may be presumed to be located as a result of observation or measurement"—Bowditch.

Local Apparent Noon (LAN). That moment when the sun crosses the observer's meridian and is at its maximum altitude for the day.

Local Hour Angle (LHA). The angular distance measured westward from the observer's meridian on the celestial sphere.

Main Arc. That part of a sextant upon which the readings in degrees are inscribed. Sometimes called the limb.

Meridian. A great circle through the geographical poles of the earth or celestial sphere. The meridian of Greenwich (0°) is called the prime meridian.

Meridian Passage (Mer Pass). The time of meridian passage; when a celestial body crosses a given meridian.

Micrometer Drum. A device for making precise, small measurements on a sextant. The mechanism is also referred to as an endless tangent screw, and a sextant so-equipped is an ETS sextant.

Navigational Triangle. The spherical triangle whose points are the elevated pole, the celestial body, and the zenith of the observer projected on earth, which is solved in determining computed altitude (Hc) and azimuth (Zn).

Noon Sight. Observation of the sun's altitude at local apparent noon.

Observed Altitude (Ho). The apparent altitude (ha) corrected for refraction (R), and in the case of the moon, additionally for horizontal parallax (H.P.).

Polar Distance. The angular distance from the celestial pole; in celestial navigation, 90° minus the declination.

Polaris. The Pole Star, located less than 1° from the North Celestial Pole in the constellation Ursa Minor. Useful for a special-case latitude determination.

Refraction (R). The correction due to the bending of light rays passing obliquely through the earth's atmosphere. The refraction correction in the *Nautical Almanac* includes, for the convenience of a single-entry solution, other elements such as semidiameter.

Semidiameter (SD). The angular distance from the center of a celestial body of finite diameter (e.g. the sun) to its outer edge or limb.

Sextant Altitude (hs). The uncorrected altitude of a celestial body as measured directly by sextant observation.

Sidereal Hour Angle (SHA). The angular distance measured westward on the celestial sphere, from the First Point of Aries through 360°.

Sight Reduction Tables. Tables for solving the navigational triangle for computed altitude (Hc) and azimuth (Zn). Pub. No. 249, *Sight Reduction Tables for Air Navigation,* is used in this text.

Standard Meridian. A central meridian selected for a time zone, located at multiples of 15° longitude east or west of Greenwich (0°).

Tabulated Altitude (Tab Hc). The uncorrected value of Hc as extracted from the sight reduction table.

Tabular Difference (d). The difference between the tabulated altitudes in a sight reduction table for successive degrees of declination. Used for purposes of interpolation.

Variable Correction (v). Small, additional corrections due to excesses of actual movement over the constant rates used in the body of the *Increments and Corrections* tables in the almanac.

Vernier. A scale for precise, small readings on a sextant.

Watch Time (W). The time registered on the navigator's watch or clock.

Zenith. That point on the celestial sphere directly over the observer.

Zenith Distance (z). The angular distance from the zenith. In celestial navigation: 90° minus the altitude—also called coaltitude.

Zone Description (ZD). The number of whole hours that are added to or subtracted from the zone time to obtain Greenwich mean time.

Index